W9-APT-056

Software Verification and Validation

A Practitioner's Guide

For a complete listing of the *Artech House Computer Science* library,
turn to the back of this book.

Software Verification and Validation

A Practitioner's Guide

Steven R. Rakitin

Artech House
Boston • London

Library of Congress Cataloging-in-Publication Data
Rakitin, Steven R.
    Software verification and validation : a practitioner's guide / Steven R. Rakitin.
       p.   cm.
    Includes bibliographical references and index.
    ISBN 0-89006-889-5 (alk. paper)
    1. Computer software—Verification.   2. Computer software—Validation.
    I. Title.
QA76.76.V47R35   1997
005.1'4—dc21   96-47264
                                                            CIP

British Library Cataloguing in Publication Data
Rakitin, Steven R.
    Software verification and validation : a practitioner's guide
    1. Computer software—Validation   2. Computer software—Verification
    I. Title
    005.1'4

    ISBN 0-89006-889-5

Cover and text design by Darrell Judd. Cover illustration by Javier Roca.

© 1997 ARTECH HOUSE, INC.
685 Canton Street
Norwood, MA 02062

International Standard Book Number: 0-89006-889-5
Library of Congress Catalog Card Number: 96-47264

10 9 8 7 6 5 4

Nothing is more precious than one's family.
To Eileen, Jason, and Sarah.
And to Pete, the best dog in the whole world.

Contents

Chapter 6

Applying the inspection process 67

About the Author   259

Index   261

Preface

Who should read this book

THIS BOOK IS FOR software quality practitioners, software engineers, and project managers who need a basic understanding of software *verification and validation* (V&V) techniques. Unfortunately, very little formal training in software V&V is offered in school. As a result, there is a gap between the skills that many software quality practitioners have and the skills they need to effectively assess the quality of software products. This book is intended for those people who are responsible for performing software V&V tasks but who have not had the luxury of receiving any training in the subject.

Why I wrote this book

The so-called software crisis was first recognized as a significant issue almost 25 years ago. The *crisis* refers to the fact that more resources were being spent on maintaining and supporting existing software than on developing new software. Attempts made to address the crisis included development of new programming languages, *computer-aided software engineering* (CASE) tools, independent V&V, and the application of formal verification methods, to name just a few. By themselves, each of these attempts had little effect.

Possibly the most significant failure that resulted from the software crisis was the failure to change the fundamental training provided to software engineers. In many universities, the software engineering curriculum is a victim of academic turf wars. Software engineering courses frequently are taught as part of electrical engineering departments and have a definite computer science bent. In 1994, the *Software Engineering Institute* (SEI) prepared a status report on undergraduate software engineering education in the United States.[1] The report's introduction stated that:

> Software engineering education in [the] United States is evolving rapidly. In the 1980s, master's-level software engineering programs were just beginning; there were few programs and their content varied considerably. The idea of a separate undergraduate software engineering program was so controversial as to be almost unimaginable. In the 1990s, master's programs are becoming more common and their content better defined. ...The idea of an undergraduate software engineering program separate from computer science, although still controversial, is being taken seriously by many people, and the first programs are being designed. By the end of the decade, we expect that software engineering degree programs at all academic levels will be well established [1].

In addition to a lack of undergraduate software engineering programs, professional organizations that represent the majority of software engineers have dragged their feet in this area as well. It was not until May 1993 that the Board of Governors of the *Institute of Electrical and Electronic Engineers* (IEEE) Computer Society considered a motion to "initiate actions to establish software engineering as a profession." In August 1993, the Council of the *Association for Computing Machinery* (ACM) similarly endorsed the establishment of a

---

1.   The SEI was established at Carnegie-Mellon University in 1984 by the U.S. Department of Defense to provide leadership in advancing the state of the practice of software engineering in order to improve the quality of systems that depend on software.

commission on software engineering. In March 1994, the IEEE Computer Society and the ACM agreed to work together on that issue [1].

In 1994, there were no universities in the United States that offered an undergraduate program leading to a bachelor of science degree in software engineering. The SEI report surveyed 11 schools that offer significant course sequences in software engineering at the undergraduate level. That only 11 schools in the United States offer a significant sequence of software engineering courses is discouraging in itself. But if we look at the courses that those 11 schools offer, we can see a larger problem.

Courses that address basic skills required to produce high-quality software products (e.g., requirements definition, software architecture and design, structured analysis and structured design, software V&V, and testing) are noticeably absent. The predominate focus of the courses offered at the 11 schools is programming.[2] One school's curriculum includes no fewer than eight different programming courses.[3] As a result of the number of programming-related courses in today's curricula, we should not be surprised by software engineering students who graduate believing that software engineers spend most of their time writing code!

Recall what Dr. Fred Brooks [2] observed over 20 years ago:

For some years, I have been successfully using the following rule of thumb for scheduling a software task:

- $\frac{1}{3}$ planning
- $\frac{1}{6}$ coding
- $\frac{1}{4}$ component test and early system test
- $\frac{1}{4}$ system test, all components in hand

---

2.   Included in the category of programming courses are those courses with the following key words in their title: *programming, data structures, numerical methods, algorithms,* and *languages.*

3.   Oregon Institute of Technology, the polytechnic institute for the Oregon State University system, has the following programming-related courses in its four-year undergraduate curriculum that leads to a B.S. in Software Engineering Technology: C Programming, Advanced C Programming, Computer Assembly Language, Advanced Assembly Language, Programming Languages II, Programming Languages III, Data Structures, and Numerical Methods.

This differs from conventional scheduling in several important ways:

1. The fraction devoted to planning is larger than normal. Even so, it is barely enough to produce a detailed and solid specification, and not enough to include research or exploration of totally new techniques.
2. The half of the schedule devoted to debugging of completed code is much larger than normal.
3. The part that is easy to estimate, i.e., coding is given only one-sixth of the schedule.

We still have not learned that requirements definition, design, and system testing require much more time (and therefore more training) than does coding. Based on my practical experience with software development projects, I believe software engineering undergraduate curricula should be changed to reflect those tasks that software engineers need to develop high-quality software.

The goal, then, of this book is to partially fill the gap between skills that have been taught and skills that are required. This book provides a source of practical, common-sense techniques and activities that can be applied to a wide range of software development projects.

How this book is organized

This book is organized into three parts. Part I contains the introduction (Chapter 1), a discussion of software lifecycle models (Chapter 2), the software development process (Chapter 3), and an economic justification for software V&V activities (Chapter 4).

Part II explores verification activities, which include the formal inspection process (described in Chapters 5 and 6), software quality metrics (Chapter 7), and configuration management (Chapter 8).

Part III examines validation activities, which include validation testing (Chapter 9), validation metrics (Chapter 10), and a discussion of software reliability growth modeling (Chapter 11).

Acknowledgments

This book would not have been possible were it not for the talented, dedicated, and quality-conscious people whom I had the distinct pleasure of working with while at Ciba Corning Diagnostics Corp. Gayle Hoffman, Robin Lamperti, Bill Mooney, Trent Lynn, William Winn, and Richard Collotta formed the nucleus of an extremely effective software quality team.

I am indebted to Len Race, who had the foresight to encourage and support the application of software V&V principles on his projects. Thanks to Keith McLain, who helped me to understand and apply the principles of software reliability growth.

Special thanks to my friend and colleague Larry Weissman, who reviewed the entire manuscript and provided me with the benefit of his software engineering wisdom.

I would also like to acknowledge the staff at Artech House for believing that this book was worth publishing. They provided a constant source of patience and encouragement.

Steven R. Rakitin
Upton, Massachusetts
January 1997

REFERENCES

[1] Ford, G., "A Progress Report on Undergraduate Software Engineering Education," CMU/SEI-94-TR-11, May 1994.

[2] Brooks, F. P., *The Mythical Man-Month*, Reading, MA: Addison-Wesley, 1975.

Part I: Introduction

THE OBJECTIVE OF Part I is to provide some context for the situation in which most software organizations find themselves. Chapter 1 provides some background on the *software crisis* and what has been and is being done about it.

Chapter 2 examines several different lifecycle models. The objective is to provide an overall framework for understanding how software V&V activities can be woven into the software development process. The discussion is continued in Chapter 3, which addresses the importance of having a written software development process.

Chapter 4 concludes Part I with an economic justification of software V&V activities.

Chapter 1

Software in perspective

We rely on software, and sometimes it fails us. Some of those failures are nuisances; some are disasters. It is not news that technology presents unique risks. Adding software to a system may make the service it provides cheaper, more generally available, or more adaptable to change, but it will not make it more reliable.

L. R. Weiner,
Digital Woes: Why We Should Not Depend on Software,
Addison-Wesley, 1993

REPLACING HARDWARE with software is one way to increase flexibility and reduce cost. But adding complex software to a product will not enhance its reliability. How does this affect critical software applications such as flight control systems on commercial airlines, patient monitoring systems, and nuclear power plant control systems? Has our need for technologically advanced products outpaced our ability to produce such products? What has the software industry done to attempt to mitigate the consequences of this situation?

1.1 The software crisis

The term *software crisis,* first used during the mid 1970s, was an acknow-
ledgment that we had exceeded our capacity to develop large, complex soft-
ware-based systems with the software development technology of the time.

It was during the mid 1970s that, for the first time, the costs of software
maintenance activities exceeded the costs of new software development. During
those same years, we saw the beginnings of what would become a significant
trend in later years: Hardware costs declined dramatically, while software costs
continued to rise and the number of software projects that failed because of
software grew substantially.

At that time, many people thought that if we only had better programming
languages, we could pull ourselves out of the crisis. Thus, the popularity of
programming languages such as PL/1, Jovial, and APL increased. But the
failures persisted.

For example, there was the error in the navigation software used in F-16s
that caused the planes to flip over when they crossed the equator. Then there
was the minuscule timing change made to the space shuttle software that caused
the launch to abort in 1981, even after thousands of hours of testing by the most
advanced software engineering team in the world. And sadly, there were at least
two deaths from radiation overdoses directly attributable to a software bug in
the Therac-25 linear accelerator [1].

In an attempt to avoid the problems associated with incorrectly translating
requirements written in English into programs, much research was focused on
formal languages for specifying requirements. Formal specification languages
(such as HAL/S) were developed to enable the creation of *natural language-
based* specifications. The idea was to develop requirements in the formal
language and then feed the formal specification to a compiler that would
translate the formal specifications directly into a traditional programming language. Much of the software originally developed for the space shuttle orbiter
was written in HAL/S.

Highly structured, multitasking programming languages (such as Modula
and Ada) were also developed to deal with those applications that had real-time,
multitasking requirements.

In practice, the impact that programming languages have on overall software reliability is relatively small compared to other factors. Programming
languages such as PL/1, Jovial, and APL are not extensively used in commercial
applications. Today, the most widely used programming languages are C, C++

and COBOL. None of these languages was developed to address software reliability issues.

1.2 No silver bullet

By 1985, the software industry had grown to over $300 billion and software engineering came to be recognized as an engineering discipline unto itself. Many companies realized that they had to make significant improvements in the process they used to develop software if they were to remain competitive.

Hardware costs continued to decline dramatically. New and powerful workstations and the networks they were part of provided the platform needed to bring CASE tools to the software engineer's desktop. CASE tools implement a specific software development process (such as Yourdon's Structured Design, Ward-Mellor, or Hatley-Pirbhai). These tools provided software engineers with the ability to represent software designs in a graphical manner that is easy to maintain, easy to cross-check, and easy to understand.

Many people (especially CASE tool vendors) believed that CASE tools represented the so-called *silver bullet* that would rescue the software industry from the software crisis. What happened instead was that many companies spent large sums of money on tools that were infrequently used. These tools implemented a process that was not consistent with the organization's software design process. We learned the hard way that there is no such thing as a *silver bullet* [2].

1.3 Attempts to resolve the software crisis

There have been many attempts to resolve the crisis, most of which have been met with little or moderate success.

1.3.1 Formal proofs of correctness

Formal proofs of correctness were an attempt to prove that programs were correct. By viewing a program as a mathematical object, it is possible to demonstrate that a program is correct in a mathematical sense. This is possible since programming languages are based on rigorous rules of syntax and semantics.

The formal proof of correction approach was most interesting to mathematicians. While it sounded good on paper, in practice its value was limited because a formal proof cannot be applied until after the code has been written. By then, it usually is too late. It was also difficult to develop proofs for large programs.

1.3.2   Independent verification and validation

The use of an independent third party (usually a separate company) to review the software development work of the prime contractor was pioneered by the *National Aeronautics and Space Administration* (NASA) and the *Department of Defense* (DoD) on mission-critical projects. The *independent V&V* (IV&V) contractor reports directly to the customer, as does the prime contractor, and usually performs a variety of tasks such as requirements analysis, requirements tracing, architecture review, design review, code inspections, and validation testing.

IV&V can be very effective, but it is prohibitively expensive on all but the most critical of applications.

1.3.3   Software quality assurance

For most software, it is not possible to justify the cost of an independent IV&V contractor. Many companies have established a *software quality assurance* (SQA) function as a sort of internal IV&V group. SQA groups typically perform many of the types of activities performed as part of an IV&V effort.

SQA has been widely accepted as being a practical, cost-effective way to improve software quality. Using an internal group, SQA has been shown to be effective in improving quality when it is applied across the entire software development process rather than as just a software testing function. However, SQA is not implemented consistently across companies, and as a result, the effectiveness of SQA varies from company to company.

1.3.4   The cleanroom process

The cleanroom process was developed by software process visionary Dr. Harlan Mills, formerly of IBM Federal Systems Division. The cleanroom process [3] combines formal program verification with *statistical process control* (SPC). In this methodology, the first priority is defect prevention through the use of mathematical proofs of correctness. *Mean time between failures* (MTBF) is used as a measure of software quality.

The cleanroom process is relatively new and has not gained wide acceptance yet. It requires significant changes in management and technical aspects of software development (specifically, knowledge of SPC as applied to software), which will further delay its acceptance.

1.4 Understanding the nature of software

Now that the Software Crisis will soon celebrate its silver anniversary, it's time we recognized that this is not a crisis, it's a situation: software has bugs. It is in its nature to have bugs, and that fact is unlikely to change soon [4].

Some significant strides have been made in the improvement of software quality and reliability. Several initiatives aimed at improving the process of software development are beginning to show positive results. Six of these initiatives are described next, just a few of the numerous software process improvement initiatives that are reshaping software engineering. Additional information on the initiatives listed here can be found on the World Wide Web.

1.4.1 SEI capability maturity model

The SEI Capability Maturity Model (CMM^{SM}) provides a basis for appraising and improving software development [5]. Through appraisals and assessments, the CMM^{SM} provides a model that organizations can use to improve their software development practices.

The CMM supports measurement of the software process by providing a framework for performing reliable and consistent appraisals. Although humans cannot be removed from the appraisal process, the CMM provides a basis for objectivity.

The CMM builds upon a set of processes and practices that have been developed in collaboration with a broad selection of practitioners.

Basing improvement efforts on a model is not without its risks, however. In the words of George Box, "All models are wrong; some models are useful." Models are simplifications of the real world they represent, and the CMM is not an exhaustive description of the software development process. It is not comprehensive; it only touches on other, nonprocess factors, such as people and technology, that affect the success of software projects [5].

In addition, the SEI has also compared the CMM^{SM} to the ISO-9000 series of standards [6] and has reported on commonly applied methods for software process improvement [7].

1.4.2 ISO SPICE

The *International Organization for Standardization*(ISO) *Software Process Improvement and Capability dEtermination* (SPICE) project is an international collaboration involving 14 nations [8, 9]. The objective is to produce a standard for software process assessment based on a rapid development program and industry trials.

The standard provides a structured approach for the assessment of software processes for the following purposes:

a) by or on behalf of an organization with the objective of understanding the state of its own processes for process improvement
b) by or on behalf of an organization with the objective of determining the suitability of its own processes for a particular requirement or class of requirements
c) by or on behalf of an organization with the objective of determining the suitability of another organization's processes for a particular contract or class of contracts.

The framework for process assessment:

a) encourages self-assessment
b) takes into account the context in which the assessed processes operate
c) produces a set of process ratings (a process profile) rather than a pass/fail result
d) through the generic practices, addresses the adequacy of the management of the assessed processes
e) is appropriate across all application domains and sizes of organizations [9]

1.4.3 Bootstrap

The Bootstrap project is a European initiative aimed at overcoming the deficiencies in the SEI CMM^{SM} [10]. The Bootstrap approach analyzes the current state of software technology used in industry and provides motivation for accepting new contexts for software engineering.

The Bootstrap methodology is fully aligned with ISO-9000 and is consistent with the SEI CMM^{SM}. However, the Bootstrap methodology provides important profiles that detail the maturity of each major aspect of software development at both an organization and individual project level.

Bootstrap was designed to accommodate diversity in approaches and methods used by software organizations in different industries. It provides a framework for evaluation based on the type of organization and its priorities and objectives and provides a detailed plan for improving the development processes and overall software quality.

1.4.4 ISO-9000-3

ISO-9000-3 provides guidance in applying the requirements of ISO-9001 (intended primarily for manufacturing organizations) for software companies. As stated in the guideline's introduction:

> ...the process of development and maintenance of software is different from that of most other types of industrial products. In such a rapidly evolving technology field it is therefore necessary to provide additional guidance for quality systems where software products are involved, taking into account the present status of this technology.

> [This guideline] deals primarily with situations where specific software is developed as part of a contract according to purchaser's specifications [11].

1.4.5 TickIT

The TickIT Guide was developed by the British Standards Institute to help customers and software development organizations improve software quality [12]. The guide includes four parts: Part A is a general introduction; Part B is the Customer's Guide; Part C is the Supplier's Guide; and Part D is the TickIT Auditor's Guide. As stated in the introduction to Part A:

> TickIT promotes the definition of processes and procedures for certification of quality systems within the context of Total Quality. Factors at work for continuous improvement include management commitment for improvement, commitment for improvement, motivation for improvement, and measures for improvement. These are not exclusive to Total Quality Management (TQM), and should be considered as forming an integral part of a quality system based on ISO-9001 [12].

1.4.6 Trillium

Trillium is a software assessment model developed by Bell Canada to assess the software product development processes of potential software suppliers in order to minimize risks and ensure timely delivery [13].

This model and its accompanying tools are not in themselves a product development process or lifecycle model. Rather, the Trillium model provides key industry practices used to improve an existing process or lifecycle.

The practices in the Trillium model are derived from a benchmarking exercise that focuses on all practices that would contribute to an organization's product development and support capability. Trillium has the following characteristics:

- It has a telecommunications orientation.
- It provides a customer focus.
- It provides a product perspective.
- It covers ISO, Bellcore, Malcolm Baldrige, IEEE, and *International Electrotechnical Commission* (IEC) standards.
- It includes technological maturity.
- It includes additional Trillium-specific practices.
- It provides a roadmap approach that sequences improvements by maturity.

1.5 Summary

The experience of the last 25 years or so has resulted in overemphasis of programming skills, to the detriment of such critical skills as requirements analysis and definition, architecture and design, and software V&V. What we have (hopefully) learned as a result of the software crisis is that the key to developing higher quality software lies in a focus on the process. As Deming observed, "The quality of a product is directly related to the quality of the process used to create it" [14].

REFERENCES

[1] Leveson, N. G, and C. S. Turner, "An Investigation of the Therac-25 Accidents," *IEEE Computer*, Vol. 26, 1993, pp. 18–41.

[2]   Brooks, F. P., "No Silver Bullet: Essence and Accidents of Software Engineering," *IEEE Computer*, April 1987, pp. 10–19.

[3]   Dyer, M., *The Cleanroom Approach to Quality Software Development*, New York: Wiley, 1992.

[4]   Weiner, L. R., *Digital Woes: Why We Should Not Depend on Software*, Reading, MA: Addison-Wesley, 1993, pp. 4–15.

[5]   Paulk, M. C., et al., *The Capability Maturity Model: Guidelines for Improving the Software Process*, Reading, MA: Addison-Wesley, 1995.

[6]   Paulk, M. C., "A Comparison of ISO 9001 and the Capability Maturity Model for Software," CMU/SEI-94-TR-12, SEI, 1994.

[7]   Austin, R., and D. Paulish, "A Survey of Commonly Applied Methods for Software Improvement," CMU/SEI-93-TR-27, SEI, 1993.

[8]   Dorling, A., "SPICE: Software Process Improvement and Capability dEtermination," *Software Quality Journal*, Vol. 2, 1993, pp. 209–224.

[9]   SPICE Consolidated Products, *Software Process Assessment - Part 1: Concepts and Introductory Guide*, Version 1.00.

[10] Haase, V., et al., "Bootstrap: Fine-Tuning Process Assessment," *IEEE Software*, July 1994, pp. 25–35.

[11] ANSI/ISO/ASQC Q-9000-3-1991, *Guidelines for the Application of ANSI/ISO/ASQC Q-9001 to the Development, Supply, and Maintenance of Software*, ASQC, 1995.

[12] *A Guide to Software Quality Management System Construction and Certification to ISO-9001 (TickIT Guide)*, Issue 3.0, British Standards Institute, 1995.

[13] Coallier, F., "TRILLIUM: A Model for the Assessment of Telecom Product Development and Support Capability," *IEEE TCSE Software Process Newsletter*, Winter 1995.

[14] Deming, W. E., *Out of the Crisis*, Cambridge: MIT Center for Advanced Engineering Study, 1982.

Chapter 2

Software development lifecycle models

S OFTWARE DEVELOPMENT organizations all follow some process when developing a software product. In immature organizations, the process usually is not written down. In mature organizations, the process is in writing and is actively managed. A key component of any software development process is the lifecycle model on which the process is based.

The particular lifecycle model used can significantly affect overall lifecycle costs associated with a software product. Many large software products are developed in one to three years, but customers may actively use those products for 10 years or even longer. As a result, costs incurred by the organization responsible for maintenance and support will be directly related to the robustness of the design and the completeness of the documentation.

This chapter reviews several software development lifecycle models to provide the context for software V&V activities and to highlight some of the strengths and weaknesses of each model.

2.1 The waterfall model

The most familiar model is the waterfall model, which is represented by Figure 2.1. During the requirements analysis phase, basic market research is performed, and potential customer requirements are identified, evaluated, and refined. The result of this phase of the process is usually a marketing requirements or product concept specification (hereafter referred to as a *concept specification*). This document is usually prepared by the product marketing group with some participation from the software engineering group. Requirements in the concept specification are usually stated in the customer's language.

The concept specification is usually written at a very high level and requires further refinement and definition for it to be useful for software development. This is the focus of the requirements definition phase of the waterfall model. Requirements in the concept specification are reviewed and analyzed by software engineers to more fully develop and refine the requirements contained in the concept specification.

Requirements from the concept specification must be restated in the software developer's language. For example, a requirement that frequently appears in concept specifications is that the software must be "user friendly." This

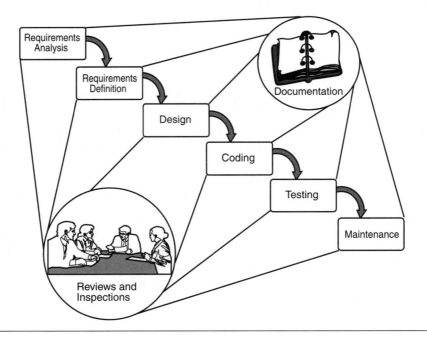

Figure 2.1   The waterfall lifecycle model.

requirement must be restated into measurable terms meaningful to software engineers, for example: "An untrained user must be able to successfully perform [some function the software provides] within [some number of] minutes." The results of the requirements definition phase is a document hereafter referred to as the *software requirements specification* (SRS) [1].

Once the SRS has been developed, software engineers should have a complete description of the requirements the software must implement. That enables software engineers to begin the design phase. In the design phase, the overall software architecture is defined, and the high-level and detailed design work is performed. This work is documented in the *software design description* (SDD) [2]

The information contained in the SDD should be sufficient to begin to the coding phase. During this phase, the design is implemented. If the SDD is complete, the coding phase proceeds smoothly, because all the information needed by the software engineers is contained in the SDD.

According to the waterfall model, the testing phase begins when the coding phase has been completed. Tests are developed based on information contained in the SRS and the SDD. These tests validate that the software meets defined requirements. A software validation test plan [3] is written to define the overall validation testing process. Individual test procedures are developed based on a logical breakdown of requirements. The testing activities are usually documented in a software validation test report. Following the successful completion of software validation testing, the product can be shipped to customers.

Once the product has been shipped, the maintenance phase begins. This phase lasts until the support for the product is discontinued. Many of the same activities performed during the development phases are also performed during the maintenance phase. It is advisable to prepare a software maintenance plan that describes how these activities are to be performed.

The waterfall model has several advantages:

- It is easy to understand.
- It is widely used.
- It reinforces the notions of "define before design" and "design before code."
- It identifies when deliverables are produced and when reviews and inspections are held.

Some of the disadvantages of the waterfall model are:

- In reality, few projects ever follow the model.

- It does not reflect the iterative nature of software development.
- It is unrealistic to expect complete and accurate requirements early in the process.
- Working software is not available until relatively late in the process, thus delaying the discovery of serious errors.
- It does not incorporate any kind of risk assessment.

2.2 The DoD-2167A model

The DoD-2167A model, shown in Figure 2.2, has been used for several years for DoD software development activities. It is similar to the waterfall model and includes additional DoD-required documents, reviews, and baselines.

There are some important differences between this model and the waterfall model. In the DoD-2167A model:

- Required documents are identified.
- Required reviews and inspections are part of the process.
- The establishment of several different baselines is included as part of the process.

Some of the advantages of this model are:

- It is well structured and well defined.
- It identifies several baselines and shows when they are created.
- It requires that interfaces be designed and documented.
- It identifies several reviews and inspections and shows when they are to be held.
- It reinforces the notions of "define before design" and "design before code."

Some of the disadvantages of the DoD-2167A model are:

- It is based on the waterfall model and therefore has the same disadvantages of that model.
- Because it is followed primarily by DoD software contractors, it uses terms and acronyms that are familiar only within the DoD community.

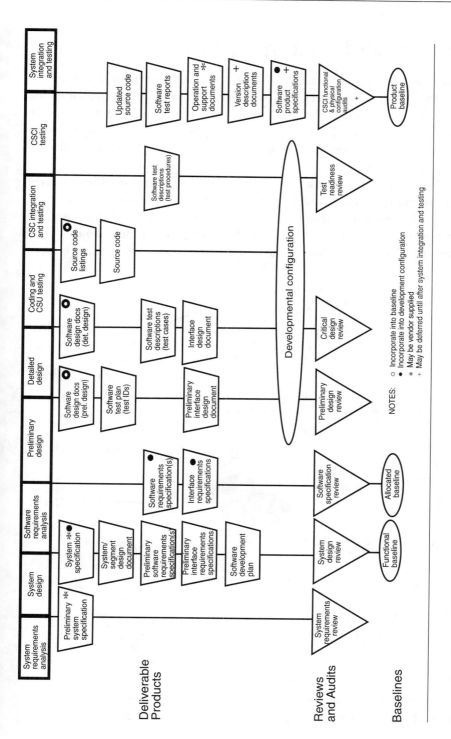

Figure 2.2 DoD-2617A software development lifecycle model [4].

2.3 The rapid prototyping model

In many instances, companies build software for customers who are not exactly sure of what they want or need. By using a prototyping approach similar to that shown in Figure 2.3, the customer can assess the prototype and provide feedback as to its suitability for the intended application. The prototype can be a paper prototype, a working system that includes both hardware and software, or anything in between.

The rapid prototyping model begins with a requirements gathering stage whereby the developers collect and refine product requirements based on whatever information is available. Then a prototype—intended to be used for requirements exploration only—is quickly developed. It is not intended to be the product. To create a prototype as quickly as possible, very little time is spent

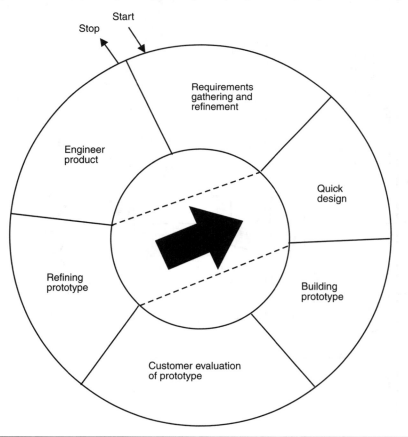

Figure 2.3   Rapid prototyping lifecycle model. (*Source:* [5], used with permission.)

developing a robust design. In addition, little or no documentation may be produced for this prototype. Customers can then evaluate and critique the prototype, providing the developers with insight to what they really want or need. Based on that evaluation, the prototype may be refined and evaluated again. This process continues until the customer and the developer agree that they have a good definition of the requirements.

The next step in the process requires that the prototype be thrown away. Now that the requirements are understood, the product can be developed using a more traditional, structured approach, such as the waterfall model.

There are some advantages of the rapid prototyping model:

- Users own the requirements, which reduces the likelihood of misunderstanding or misinterpretation.
- The developers are confident that they are building the right product.
- For those situations in which customers do not know exactly what they need, this model provides a means of requirements discovery.

Some of the disadvantages of this model are:

- Frequently, the prototype is not thrown away and becomes the product. Depending on how the prototype was developed, this can result in major problems for long-term support and maintenance of the product.
- This model requires extensive participation and involvement of the customer, which is not always possible.
- Software validation is difficult because requirements usually are not well documented.

2.4 The spiral model

The spiral model attempts to build on the benefits of the rapid prototyping model and traditional structured development models, such as the waterfall model. The spiral model, developed by Boehm and shown in Figure 2.4, adds two new concepts to software development models: risk analysis and cost.

The spiral model can be viewed as consisting of four basic activities, which correspond to the four quadrants of Figure 2.4:

- Planning;
- Risk analysis;

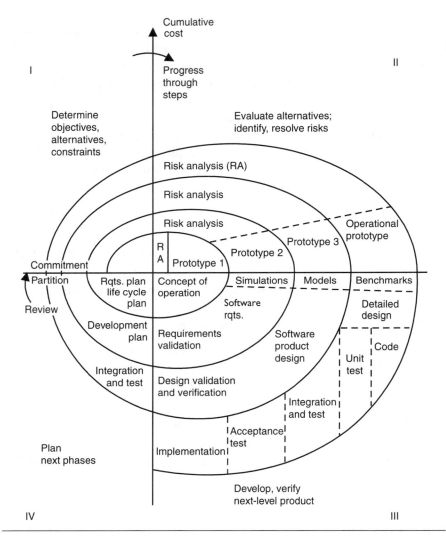

Figure 2.4   Spiral lifecycle model. (*Source:* [6]. © 1988 IEEE.)

- Development;
- Assessment.

The radial dimension of Figure 2.4 represents increasing costs. Each path around the spiral is indicative of increased costs. Also, many of the same activities are repeated during each trip around the spiral, which reflects the iterative nature of software development.

During the first trip around the spiral, planning is performed, risks are analyzed, prototypes are built, and customers evaluate the prototype. Table 2.1 includes a summary by Boehm of the most commonly encountered risks and his suggested risk management techniques [6].

Table 2.1   Commonly Encountered Risks and Risk Management Techniques

Risk	Risk Management Technique
Personnel shortfalls	Staffing with top talent; job matching; team building; cross-training; prescheduling; key people; morale building
Unrealistic schedules and budgets	Detailed, multisource cost and schedule estimation; design to cost; incremental development; software reuse; requirements scrubbing
Developing the wrong software functions	Organization analysis; mission analysis; operational-concept formulation; user surveys; prototyping; early users' manuals
Developing the wrong user interface	Task analysis; prototyping; scenarios; user characterization (functionality, style, workload)
Gold plating	Requirements scrubbing; prototyping; cost-benefit analysis; design to cost
Continuing stream of requirement changes	High change threshold; information hiding; incremental development (deferral of changes to later increments)
Shortfalls in externally furnished components	Benchmarking; inspections; reference checking; compatibility analysis
Shortfalls in externally performed tasks	Reference checking; preaward audits; award-fee contracts; competitive design or prototyping; team building
Real-time performance shortfalls	Simulation; benchmarking; modeling; prototyping; instrumentation; tuning
Straining computer-science capabilities	Technical analysis; cost-benefit analysis; prototyping; reference checking

During the second trip around the spiral, a more refined prototype is built, requirements are documented and validated, and customers are involved in assessing the new prototype.

By the time the third trip around begins, risks are known, and a somewhat more traditional development approach is taken.

The spiral model has two distinct advantages:

- Because the model incorporates the iterative nature of software development, it represents the most realistic approach.

- It incorporates the advantages of both the waterfall model and the rapid prototyping model.

Some disadvantages of the spiral model are:

- It requires expertise in risk analysis.
- If a significant risk is overlooked, major problems could result.
- The model is not well understood by nontechnical management and is not widely used.

2.5 Hybrid models

Hybrid models are combinations of aspects of two or more models. Many hybrid models, such as the one shown in Figure 2.5, are based on so-called *fourth-generation techniques* (4GT), which consist of a wide array of tools that enable software engineers to depict software characteristics at a very high level.

In those instances where requirements are reasonably well known, developers can follow the leftmost path of the model. Where requirements are not well known, developers can employ the rapid prototyping techniques. Hybrid models allow developers the flexibility to pick and choose the development model that best suits the particular situation.

Some of the advantages of a hybrid model are:

- It enables developers to choose the model that best fits the situation.
- It has all the advantages of each model it encompasses.

Some of the disadvantages are:

- Because it is a flexible combination of other models designed to suit a particular situation, a hybrid model will not be widely understood or recognized.

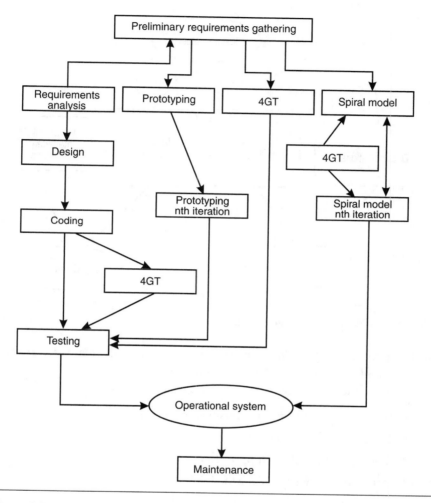

Figure 2.5 Fourth-generation lifecycle model. (*Source:* [5], used with permission.)

- A hybrid model has all the disadvantages of each model it encompasses.

2.6 Model-based development

Several model-based development approaches have recently been introduced to help design and implement client-server applications and applications based on a *graphical user interface* (GUI). An example of model-based development

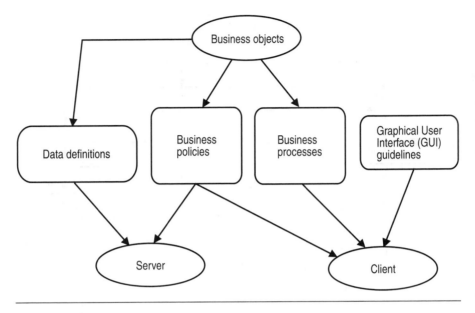

Figure 2.6 Model-based development.

is shown in Figure 2.6. This approach is most applicable to a wide variety of business and *information systems* (IS) software.

Some of the advantages of the model-based development approach are:

- It is closely tied to specific business processes.
- It clearly delineates client and server applications.
- Tools are available to support the use of the models.
- It includes a style guide for the GUI.

Some of the disadvantages of this approach are:

- It does not include a structured development approach.
- It does not reference specific documents, deliverables, or reviews.

Further information on model-based development is available from the SEI [7].

2.7 Object-oriented models

When object-oriented (OO) techniques first appeared, the emphasis was on programming languages, followed by design and, later, analysis. Recently, attention has focused on OO lifecycle methodologies. While this work is still evolving, a few OO methodologies are currently being used. Most of these methodologies emphasize the incremental, iterative, and concurrent nature of software development. Since classes and objects are used throughout the OO software development lifecycle, the process is often referred to as:

> ...seamless, meaning there is no conceptual gap between the phases as is often the case with other software development methodologies, such as the analysis (using Data Flow Diagrams) to design (structure charts) to programming gaps found in traditional structured analysis and design. Seamlessness together with naturalness is a big advantage for consistency [8].

An example of a recently developed OO methodology is Fusion. Fusion is a software development methodology for OO software developed at Hewlett-Packard Laboratories in Bristol, England, by Coleman et al. [9,10]. The method divides the software development process into phases (analysis, design, and implementation) and identifies what should be done in each phase. It provides guidance on ordering tasks within phases and criteria that can be used to decide when to move on to the next phase.

During the analysis phase, the intended behavior of the system is analyzed by developing models that describe the following:

- Classes of objects that exist in the system;
- Relationships between those classes;
- Operations that can be performed on the system;
- Allowable sequences of those operations.

During the design phase, different ways of breaking up an operation into interactions can be examined, and operations are attached to classes. Also established during this phase is how objects refer to each other and what the appropriate inheritance relationships are between classes. Design models are developed to show:

- How operations on the system are implemented by interacting objects;
- How classes refer one to another and how they are related by inheritance;
- The attributes of and operations performed on classes.

The implementation phase turns the design into code in a particular programming language. For example,

- Inheritance, reference, and class attributes are implemented in programming-language classes.
- Object interactions are encoded as methods belonging to a selected class.
- The permitted sequences of operations are recognized by state machines.

Because this methodology has been developed only recently, the advantages and disadvantages are yet to be determined.

2.8 Summary

Choosing a software lifecycle model is a difficult task. The lifecycle model can have far-reaching implications that go well beyond the software development process itself and extend into the product support and maintenance phase. Recall that the lifetime of a typical software product can be from two to five times as long as the development time. The ability of your maintenance and support organization to provide cost-effective software updates and feature enhancements is directly related to the lifecycle model and the software development process used to develop the product.

REFERENCES

[1] ANSI/IEEE Standard 830-1984, *IEEE Guide to Software Requirements Specifications*, 1984, IEEE, Inc., 345 East 47th Street, NY, NY 10017.

[2] ANSI/IEEE Standard 1016-1987, *IEEE Recommended Practice for Software Design Descriptions*, 1987, IEEE, Inc., 345 East 47th Street, NY, NY 10017.

[3] ANSI/IEEE Standard 1012-1986, *IEEE Standard for Software Verification and Validation Plans*, 1986, IEEE, Inc. 345 East 47th Street, NY, NY 10017.

[4] U.S. Department of Defense, DOD-STD-2167A, *Military Standard - Defense System Software Development*, NAVMAT 09Y, Feb. 29, 1988, Washington, D.C., pp. 12, 13.

[5]   Pressman, R., *Software Engineering: A Practitioner's Approach*, 3rd Ed., New York: McGraw-Hill, 1992, pp. 27.

[6]   Boehm, B., "A Spiral Model for Software Development and Enhancement," *IEEE Computer,* Vol. 21, 1988, pp. 61–72.

[7]   Withey, J. V. "Implementing Model Based Software Engineering in Your Organization: An Approach to Domain Engineering" *CMU/SEI-94-TR-01*, Carnegie-Mellon University, Pittsburgh: SEI, 1994.

[8]   Object-orientation FAQ, located on the World Wide Web, which at the time of publication could be found at http://iamwww.unibe.ch/~scg/ooinfo/faq.

[9]   Coleman, D., et. al., *Object-Oriented Development: The Fusion Method,* Englewood Cliffs, NJ: Prentice Hall, 1994.

[10] A description of the fusion method written by D. Coleman appeared on the Hewlett-Packard Labs Web page, which at the time of publication was located at http://www.hp l.hp/fusion.

Chapter 3

The software development process

OR A MANUFACTURING COMPANY, the key to improving the quality of its products is controlling variation. Controlling variation is achieved by having well-defined processes and by measuring actual variation. In a manufacturing environment, a typical example of variation is tolerance. To control tolerance to an acceptable level, control limits are established. If the tolerance exceeds the established limits, a root cause analysis is performed to determine why the limits were exceeded. As a result of the root cause analysis, corrective action is implemented, which results in changes to the process or adjustments to the control limits. Additional steps may be added to ensure that the tolerance requirement is met.

The three basic steps in the manufacturing process are:

1. The process is defined.
2. Product is produced by following the process.
3. The product is constantly evaluated to ensure that it conforms to established requirements.

Results of evaluations are used to drive process improvement. This concept is known as the Shewart cycle or the plan-do-check-act (PDCA) cycle and is shown in Figure 3.1. It was developed by Walter Shewart in the 1920s and put into practice as a result of the work of Deming [1,2].

For software companies, one of the keys to improving quality is applying the principles of the Shewart cycle. Controlling variation— the variations between software engineers as well as variations from one project to another—is a challenge faced by most software development organizations. Software organizations that are known for the high quality of their software products (such as Hewlett-Packard, Motorola, and AT&T, to name a few) have learned how to measure and control variation. These organizations all have well-defined software development processes.

Issues regarding the software development process and its significance in improving software are presented here in the form of *frequently asked questions*

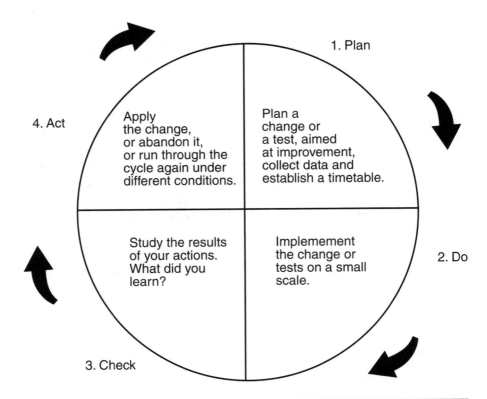

Figure 3.1   The Shewart cycle.

(FAQs). An example of a written software development process based on the waterfall model is included in Appendix G. Outlines of some of the deliverables called out by this process are included in Appendix H.

3.1 Software development process FAQs

Why is it important that the process be written?

A key attribute of a good process is that it is written. If the process is written, it can be read, understood, questioned, communicated, modified, and, most important, improved. It is not possible to do all that when the process exists in someone's head. Writing down the process makes good business sense.

Much of the recent work in software quality and software process improvement has been focused on capability assessments (SEI CMM[SM] [3] and SPICE [4]), supplier capabilities (ISO [5], TickIT [6], and TRILLIUM [7]), and software process improvement (Bootstrap [8]). A written development process is a common thread that appears throughout all these initiatives.

Won't a written process stifle creativity?

This concern is unfounded and stems from a lack of understanding of what a process is. A written process defines the mechanics of developing software. It does not define *how* software engineers do what they do. In fact, it can be argued that a good process allows software engineers more time to be creative since they don't have to spend time thinking about the more mundane aspects of their job (like what information needs to be included in an SDD document).

In every other engineering discipline, processes and procedures have been developed based on good engineering practice and years of experience. Those processes and procedures enable engineers to focus more of their time on developing creative and innovative products in a manner that ensures that the product can be successfully developed, manufactured, supported, and maintained. Written processes and procedures used in other engineering disciplines have not stifled creativity.

As experience is gained from developing products, it can be factored into the process so developers can learn from past mistakes and achieve continuous process improvement. A written software development process provides a mechanism for building on past experiences and avoiding making the same costly mistakes. A written process is a characteristic of mature software organizations and can have a significant effect on quality, development cost, schedule, and time to market.

We have a process that isn't written down, but it seems to work. Why should we change it?

If you have an unwritten process that seems to work, then why not write it down? Putting a process on paper in no way changes the process. Writing the process down will, however, make it easier to:

- Train new people in how your organization develops software;
- Improve product quality by making process improvements based on past mistakes and experience;
- Identify those areas where improvements are needed.

How can I convince the software engineering manager to follow a written procedure?

Some managers like working in an environment where the process is undefined and undocumented. Unfortunately, that often leads to inefficiency and less-than-stellar product quality. So how do you convince someone to follow a written process? One way that seems to work is to build a case based on cost. Collect data from past projects that show the time and effort spent developing, testing, and debugging the software. Examples of metrics to collect are:

- Total lines of source code developed;
- Total software engineering person-hours spent;
- Number of bugs identified prerelease;
- Number of bugs identified postrelease;
- Total effort spent developing and executing tests;
- Find and fix times for bugs found prerelease;
- Find and fix times for bugs found postrelease.

Then propose that the software engineering manager and someone who represents the software quality group work together on developing a flexible process to use on the next project. The goal would be to make improvements based on the metrics you collected from past projects. The key is to work collaboratively and remain flexible. Compromise may be the best solution.

How can having a written process improve software quality?

A written software development process will not improve quality alone. It must:

- Be followed by everyone;
- Be flexible and changeable;
- Include metrics that measure process effectiveness and form the basis for changes to the process;
- Be actively managed.

Once a software development process is in place, some intangible benefits may be realized:

- It helps connect software engineering to other engineering disciplines within the *research and development* (R&D) organization.
- It helps establish a corporate memory on software development so the organization can learn from past mistakes.
- It helps improve the use of valuable resources by providing a mechanism for learning from others; allowing software engineers to spend more time solving problems that require their creative energy; reducing rework and allowing software engineers to move on to new projects sooner; and providing a training tool for new software engineers.
- It can increase the likelihood of successfully introducing new technology.
- It provides consistency and lowers overall costs.
- It provides a framework for continuous process improvement (PDCA cycle).

An extensive list of resources related to software process improvement can be found in the *Software Process Newsletter* [9], as well as on the SEI's home page on the World Wide Web.

We do not have a written procedure (or we have one but do not follow it), and the quality of our software is not too bad. Why should we change?

Customers will tolerate software that "is not too bad" for just so long. Companies that develop leading edge technology typically have groups of customers called "early adopters," who are willing to accept lower quality software but only for a relatively short time. As the leading edge technology becomes more widely accepted and integrated into competitors' products, the early adopters become more mainstream customers. Product quality is a key factor in retaining the base of mainstream customers.

Consumers tend to tell many more people about an unhappy experience with a product than they tell about a happy one. The same holds for software.

What is *software quality* anyway?

Watts Humphrey observed that:

> The principal focus of any software quality definition should be user's needs. Crosby defines quality as "conformance to requirements" [10]. While one can debate the distinction between requirements, needs, and wants, quality definitions must consider the users' perspective. The key questions then are, who are the users, what is important to them, and how do their priorities relate to the way you build, package, and support your products?" [11]

Knowing your customers, what they need, and how they use your products is all part of the intangible attributes that collectively lead to a qualitative assessment of software quality. As will be discussed in Chapter 9, knowing your customers and how they use your products can play a key role in helping developers test software more effectively.

There are several quantitative ways to measure software quality. One good example is the software defect removal efficiency developed by Capers Jones [12]. The software defect removal efficiency is defined by counting the number of defects found prior to the release of a product and dividing it by the total number of defects found. The total number of defects found is the sum of those the developer finds and the number reported by customers during the first n months of actual use. Best-in-class companies like Hewlett-Packard, Motorola, IBM, and AT&T have a defect-removal efficiency of 99%. Most typical software companies are in the range of 70% to 75%. A more thorough discussion of software quality measures can be found in the SEI report on software quality measurement [13].

So we take the process that we currently use and write it down. Then what?

That depends on the organization. Is your organization satisfied with the quality (however it defines "quality") of the software it produces? Are the customers satisfied? Do customers typically report only a few bugs during the first few months following the release of a new software product or version? Are the organization's products perceived to be significantly better than competitors' products? If the answer to these questions is, "No," then your organization needs to look at ways it can improve the perceived quality of its products. Having a written process will help. Collect some process and product data that documents where the organization currently is product quality—wise, then make some process changes (e.g., require that an SDD be written before coding begins or institute code inspections) and see how those changes affect product quality.

How can you build in flexibility so that the process can be tailored to suit the needs of the project team?

The software development process should be viewed as a guideline. A part of each project should be a written software development project plan. The purpose of the plan is to define in detail the specific tasks, activities, deliverables, and tools that will be required for the project. That way, the software development process can be tailored to meet the specific needs of each project.

Deviations from the software development process need to be justified based on good engineering judgment. Management, the product support group, and the quality group should be required to agree to all deviations from the software development process. In that way, flexibility can be achieved in a manner that still retains appropriate checks and balances.

How can information collected from using the process be used to improve the process?

By careful selection of a set of appropriate process and product metrics, the data can be used to improve process and product quality. For example, the data collected on the types of defects found during code inspections (an example of a process metric) can be used to revise the organization's coding standards. Once common problems have been reflected in the coding standards, they are much less likely to occur in the future. Similarly, data collected on the types of problems reported by customers (an example of a product metric) can be used to change the software validation test suite to be more representative of actual customer use of the product. Including such tests in the test suite will increase the likelihood that similar types of problems will be caught and corrected before the product is released.

Who should be responsible for enforcing the process?

Ideally, there should be no need for enforcement. Everyone should understand the value to the company derived by following the process. When the process is "owned" by the software development team (i.e., software engineers were actively involved in developing the process), enforcement is not an issue. When software engineers are not involved in developing the process, enforcement is an issue.

Management has the responsibility for ensuring that the process is followed. The quality group may have oversight in this area, but viewing the quality staff as "enforcers" diminishes their effectiveness in achieving the company's overall quality objectives.

Who should be the keeper of the process?

It is important that the mechanism for changing the software development process be clearly defined. Ideally, this responsibility should be shared by those who are bound to follow it in a manner that allows for input, discussion, assessment, and revision in a timely and controlled manner. Ownership is key. In many forward-thinking, quality-conscious organizations, management owns the process.

3.2 Summary

A written software development process is essential for organizations to make significant improvements in software quality. The process needs to be written so it can be read, understood, communicated, followed, and, most importantly, improved. Having a written software development process allows software V&V activities to be woven into the fabric that defines a company's software development culture.

Ownership of the process is vitally important. Ownership will go a long way in ensuring that the process is followed. Measuring the effectiveness of the software development process should be standard practice. Collected data can be used to drive improvements to the process. This approach is based on the principles of statistical process control, which have been successfully applied in many other engineering and manufacturing disciplines.

REFERENCES

[1]   Shewart, W., *Statistical Methods From the Viewpoint of Quality Control*, Graduate School, U.S. Dept. of Agriculture, Washington, 1939; Dover, 1968.

[2] Deming, W. E., *Out of the Crisis*, Cambridge: MIT Center for Advanced Engineering Study, 1982.

[3] Paulk, M. C., et al., *The Capability Maturity Model: Guidelines for Improving the Software Process*, Reading, MA: Addison-Wesley, 1995.

[4] Dorling, A., "SPICE: Software Process Improvement and Capability dEtermination," *Software Quality Journal*, Vol. 2, 1993, pp. 209–224.

[5] ANSI/ISO/ASQC Q-9000-3-1991, *Guidelines for the Application of ANSI/ISO/ASQC Q-9001 to the Development, Supply, and Maintenance of Software*, ASQC, 1995.

[6] *A Guide to Software Quality Management System Construction and Certification to ISO-9001 (TickIT Guide)*, Issue 3.0, October 1995, British Standards Institute, 1995.

[7] Coallier, F., "TRILLIUM: A Model for the Assessment of Telecom Product Development and Support Capability," *IEEE TCSE Software Process Newsletter*, Winter 1995.

[8] Haase, V., et al., "Bootstrap: Fine-Tuning Process Assessment," *IEEE Software*, July 1994, pp. 25–35.

[9] El Emam, K., ed., *Software Process Newsletter*, published by IEEE TCSE, No. 2, Winter 1995.

[10] Crosby, P., *Quality Is Free: The Art of Making Quality Certain*, New York: Mentor, New American Library, 1979.

[11] Humphrey, W. S., *A Discipline for Software Engineering*, Reading, MA: Addison-Wesley, 1995.

[12] Jones, C., "Software Defect-Removal Efficiency," *IEEE Computer*, Vol. 29, No. 4, April 1996, pp. 94–95.

[13] Florac, W., "Software Quality Measurement: A Framework for Counting Problems and Defects," *CMU/SEI-TR-92-022*, SEI, 1992.

Chapter 4

Economic justification

Most American executives think they are in business to make money, rather than products and services like computers, steels, autos, semiconductors, and banking. The Japanese corporate credo, on the other hand, is that a company should become the world's most efficient provider of whatever product and service it offers. Once it becomes the world leader and continues to offer good products and services, profits follow.

Y. Tsurumi,
"Instruction for U. S. Management: Japanese Competition Can Be Healthy,"
New York Times, May 1983

THE QUOTATION FROM Yoshi Tsurumi, professor and director of the Pacific Basin Economic Study Center at UCLA, illustrates a serious problem with management in many Western companies. Too often, the need of shareholders for quarterly results overshadows the needs of customers. While shareholder confidence is important, many organizations fail to recognize that customers keep the business running, not shareholders.

In most organizations, the pressure to get products to market as quickly as possible is intense. Development processes that once took two to three years are being compressed to one year or less. In some markets, software products are updated ("refreshed" is the current marketing term) and released every six months. As a result, many organizations are looking for ways to streamline the development process to meet increasing market pressures.

In today's highly competitive, global economy, successful organizations have learned to make tradeoffs between time to market and time to profit. Time to market is a well-understood concept, whereas time to profit is not as well understood. Both approaches are illustrated in Figure 4.1.

Time to profit is the time from when a product is released to the break-even point, the point at which the revenue stream generated by sales of the product exceeds the cost of maintaining and supporting the product.

When the software development organization focuses solely on time-to-market goals, the quality of the product frequently suffers. Releasing a low-quality product usually results in higher maintenance and support costs and unhappy customers. The break-even point occurs much later (if at all).

Alternatively, if the software development organization is geared toward achieving time-to-profit goals, the quality of the product usually is much better, thus reducing overall maintenance and support costs. Lower maintenance and support costs mean happier customers. The break-even point occurs much sooner, which means higher profits. In a highly competitive marketplace, organizations need to make informed decisions regarding the balance between achieving time-to-market and time-to-profit goals.

This chapter discusses the economic justification for performing software V&V activities. Understanding the economics of software V&V is crucial to understanding how an organization can make these tradeoffs.

4.1 Economic justification

Organizations perform certain activities as part of the software development process because management believes such activities are economically justified. For example, organizations may send software engineers to training courses to learn new programming techniques, such as *object-oriented design* (OOD) or to learn how to use CASE tools that support OOD. The training costs (both the cost of the training and the time spent at training sessions) can be economically justified by management based on the return they are likely to provide in terms

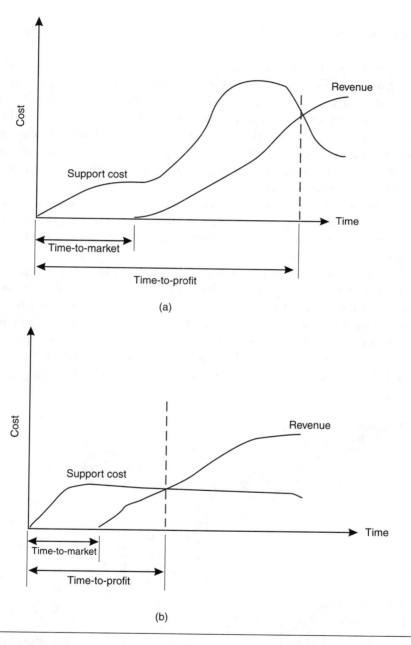

(a)

(b)

Figure 4.1 (a) Time-to-market approach and (b) time-to-profit approach. (*Adapted from:* [1].)

of improved product design, lower development and maintenance costs, and so on.

Organizations may spend considerable amounts of time and money performing activities like rapid prototyping and conjoint analysis [2] and using techniques such as *quality function deployment* (QFD) [3–5] to identify customer requirements with a high degree of certainty. For all these activities, there is a return on investment. Software engineers learn new skills that will help them produce better products in less time. Marketing people learn what the customer really wants. And customers get a higher quality product that meets their needs in the time frame they require.

Like any other activity, software V&V activities need to be justified economically. Not surprisingly, a cost is associated with performing those activities. However, there is also a cost associated with *not* performing the activities. The question is which cost is greater.

Several studies have been performed to try to answer that question. A landmark study by Boehm [6] reported that the cost to find and fix defects found during the software development process increased significantly the later the defect was found. As illustrated in Figure 4.2, the relative cost to find and fix a defect found during the requirements definition phase increases by a factor of 50 times that amount if the same defect is not found until the testing phase and to a factor of 100 times if not found until after the product has been shipped.

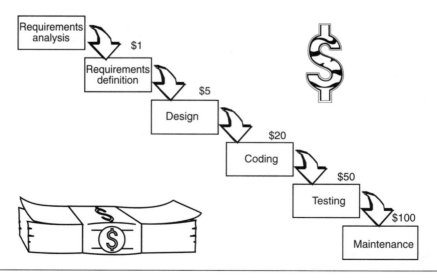

Figure 4.2   Relative cost factor to find and fix defects [6].

A similar study by Good [7] reported that a defect that cost $350 to find and fix during the requirements definition phase can cost more than $12,000 to find and fix if not detected until the testing phase. Other cost data summarized by Humphrey [8] are consistent with that reported by Boehm and Good.

Costs associated with software quality are typically incurred as a result of software V&V activities, including defect-detection, removal, and prevention activities. The costs associated with performing those activities are relatively straightforward and easy to measure. For example, costs associated with performing requirements, design, and code inspections, developing and executing software validation tests, and other similar software V&V tasks are relatively simple to determine.

Costs resulting from not performing those activities are, however, not so straightforward and easy to measure. How do you measure the cost of customer dissatisfaction resulting from poor-quality software? How do you measure lost sales resulting from failure to deliver a product on time because it had so many bugs that it had to be reworked several times? While it may be difficult to measure those costs, it is important to collect the information so that organizations can make appropriate decisions regarding the specific software V&V activities it makes sense to perform. Once the costs are identified and measured, they can be used to help drive process improvements that can lead to lower development costs, shorter time to market, and higher customer satisfaction.

4.2 Software defect cost models

Developing a software defect cost model can help identify the costs associated with software defects. The model should identify costs associated with software development, documentation, testing, and so on, prior to release to customers (prerelease) as well as costs incurred after the software is released (postrelease). An example of such a model is illustrated by the diagram shown in Figure 4.3.

A more detailed look at costs associated with software defects is the defect removal cycle. This cycle represents the activities associated with removing (finding and fixing) defects both prerelease and postrelease. Typical defect removal cycles are shown in Figures 4.4 and 4.5. Activities are identified based on the tasks that are performed when a defect is found in the product. Modeling the defect removal process and measuring the time to complete the process is important to help justify software V&V activities.

Once the data have been collected, they can be presented in a form similar to those shown in Tables 4.1 and 4.2. Some assumptions are made:

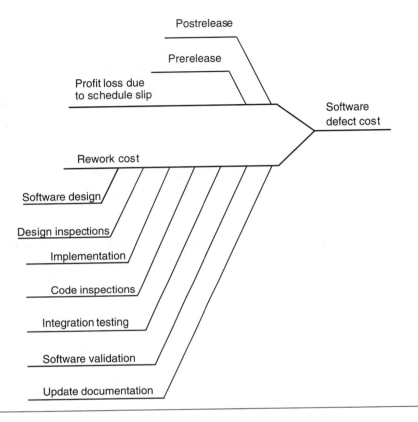

Figure 4.3   Software defect cost model [9].

- Empirical data support the range of defect removal time of 10–30 hours per defect prerelease [8,10] and 20–60 hours per defect postrelease. These time estimates include all the activities shown in Figures 4.4 and 4.5.

- A staff cost figure of $75 per hour is an average for software engineers and includes salary, benefits, overhead, and so on. Substitute your actual costs here.

- The number of defects to be removed varies from project to project and from company to company. Substitute actual numbers you have gathered from past projects.

- The postrelease defect removal time is higher because of the additional tasks required (see Figure 4.5). These costs do not include the costs associated with scrapping inventory of a defective product and reissuing an updated software release to customers.

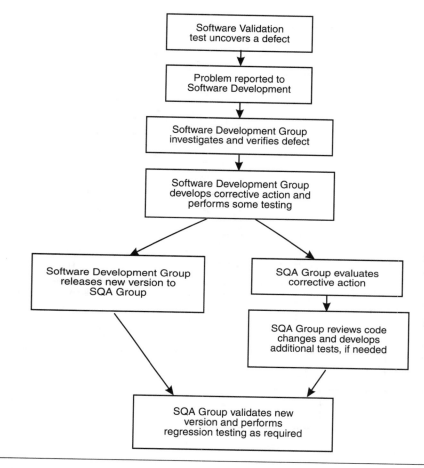

Figure 4.4   Prerelease find/fix cycle.

Pressman [11] suggests that the cost of performing software V&V activities can be economically justified if:

$$C3 > C1 + C2$$

where:

> $C3$ = cost of defects without software V&V activity
> $C1$ = actual costs of software V&V activities
> $C2$ = cost of defects not found by software V&V

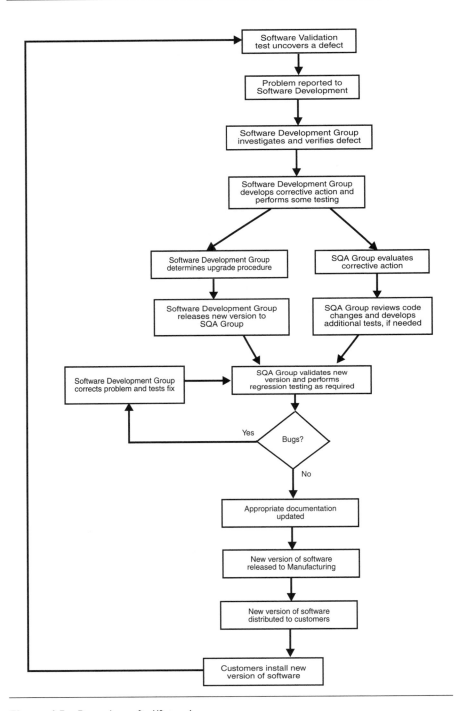

Figure 4.5   Postrelease find/fix cycle.

Table 4.1 Typical Prerelease Defect Removal Costs

Find/Fix Time (Hours/Defect)	Staff Cost ($/Hour)	Number of Defects To Be Removed	Defect Removal Cost
10	$75	100	$75,000
30	$75	300	$675,000

Table 4.2 Typical Postrelease Defect Removal Costs

Find/Fix Time (Hours/Defect)	Staff Cost ($/Hour)	Number of Defects To Be Removed	Defect Removal Cost
20	$75	50	$75,000
60	$75	200	$900,000

Estimate $C3$ using historical data from previous projects that did not have software V&V. Estimate $C1$ using the cost of people and equipment on similar projects that did have software V&V. Estimate $C2$ using the postrelease defect removal model and the number of defects found by customers.

4.3 Measuring the cost of quality

Juran described the cost-of-quality measure as a way to "quantify the size of the quality problem in language that will have impact on upper management" [12].

The cost-of-quality measurement comprises the following three activities:

- Detection, which focuses on tasks that help find defects;
- Prevention, which is centered around tasks that help prevent defects from occurring in the first place;
- Removal, which includes a variety of tasks related to the isolation and correction of bugs, the verification of bug fixes, and the costs associated with preparing distribution media and redistributing software.

Examples of prevention, detection, and removal tasks are given in Table 4.3.

Table 4.3   Examples of Defect Prevention, Detection, and Removal Tasks

Defect Prevention	Defect Detection	Defect Removal
Training	Inspections	Fault isolation
Planning	Testing	Fault analysis
Simulation	Auditing	Root cause analysis
Modeling	Monitoring	Software modifications
Consulting	Measuring	Document modifications
Qualifying	Verification	Test modifications
Certifying	Validation	Regression testing
Process improvements	Requirements tracing	Rework inspections
Configuration management		Problem tracking
.	.	Scrap and rework of media
.	.	Duplication and distribution
.	.	.
.	.	.
.	.	.

The motivation for measuring the cost of quality is to use this information to convince management that it is more cost-effective to spend time and effort on detection and prevention-related activities than on removal activities.

4.4 Summary

When a complex device is being built, it is logical to expect that the sooner a defect is found, the less expensive it is to correct. The same logic applies to software. The evidence overwhelmingly indicates that the sooner defects in requirements, design, and code are found, the easier and less expensive they are to fix.

When a software team starts a new project, typically there is an initial desire among the team to "do things right this time." This desire is usually strongest during the early stages of the project. However, as reality begins to set in and the team realizes it cannot meet the unrealistic schedules imposed on them, something has to give. More often than not, what goes are software V&V activities. It is amazing how often we seem to not have the time to do it right but do seem to have the time to do it over and over and over.

Additional references on software economics can be found in SEI's Annotated Bibliography on the World Wide Web (at the time of publication, http://www.sei.cmu.edu) [13–15].

REFERENCES

[1] Fujimura, Akira, "Software Engineering Needs a Zero Defect Culture," *Computer Design*, September 1993, pp. 78–79.

[2] Cattin, P., and R. R. Wittink, "Commercial Use of Conjoint Analysis: A Survey," *Journal of Marketing*, Vol. 46, No. 3, 1982, pp. 44–53.

[3] Hauser, J. R., and D. Clausing, "The House of Quality," *Harvard Business Review*, No. 3, May–June 1988, pp. 63–73.

[4] Lamia, W. M., "Integrating QFD With Object Oriented Software Design Methodologies," *Transactions From the Seventh Symposium on Quality Function Deployment*, June 1995, pp. 417–434.

[5] Zultner, R. E., "Quality Function Deployment (QFD) for Software: Structured Requirements Exploration," in G. G. Schulmeyer and J. I. McManus, eds., *Total Quality Management for Software*, New York: Van Nostrand Reinhold, 1992.

[6] Boehm, B. W., *Software Engineering Economics*, Englewood Cliffs, NJ: Prentice-Hall, 1981.

[7] Good, D. L., "Cost-Effectiveness," *ACM Software Engineering Notes*, Vol. 11, No. 11, 1986, p. 82.

[8] Humphrey, W. S., *A Discipline for Software Engineering*, Reading, MA: Addison-Wesley, 1995, pp. 275–277.

[9] Ward, J., "Calculating the Real Cost of Software Defects," *Proc. 27th Ann. Conf. Assoc. for the Advancement of Medical Instrumentation (AAMI)*, 1992.

[10] Humphrey, W. S., *Managing the Software Process*, Reading, MA: Addison-Wesley, 1989, p. 12.

[11] Pressman, R., *Software Engineering: A Practitioner's Approach*, 3rd Ed., New York: McGraw-Hill, 1992, pp. 587–588.

[12] Juran, J. M., and F. M. Gryna, *Juran's Quality Control Handbook,* 4th Ed., New York: McGraw-Hill, 1988.

[13] Boehm, B., and P. Papaccio, "Understanding and Controlling Software Costs," *IEEE Transactions on Software Engineering,* October 1988.

[14] Geringer, P., and W. Hutzler, *Analytical Methods in Software Engineering Economics*, New York: Springer-Verlag, 1994.

[15] Wellman, F., *Software Costing*, Englewood Cliffs, NJ: Prentice-Hall, 1992.

Part II: Overview of software verification activities

Verification and validation are two distinctly different sets of activities. Yet, many people often use the terms interchangeably. So, let us clarify what is meant by verification and what is meant by validation. *Verification* can be defined as:

The process of determining whether or not the products of a given phase of the software development cycle fulfill the requirements established during the previous phase [1].

Verification activities are in-process activities performed concurrently with software development. Another way to view verification activities is that verification helps answer this question: "Are we building the product *right*?" Verification activities are discussed in detail in Chapters 5 through 8.

Validation can be defined as:

The process of evaluating software at the end of the software development process to ensure compliance with software requirements [1].

Verification activities are defined around three basic processes: inspection, measurement, and configuration management. Chapters 5 and 6 introduce the inspection process and describe how it can be applied to perform requirements, design, code, and test inspections. An extensive collection of supporting materials for the inspection process are included in the appendixes.

Chapter 7 discusses the measurement process. The process of implementing a software measurement program is examined, along with examples of specific metrics that support software V&V activities.

Chapter 8 takes up the configuration management process and discusses tasks related to identification, baseline management, and auditing and reporting.

Validation activities are performed after the software has been developed to determine if the software correctly implements the requirements. Another way to view validation activities is that validation helps answer this question: "Did we build the *right* product?" Validation activities are discussed in detail in Part III (Chapters 9 through 11).

REFERENCE

[1]   ANSI/IEEE Standard 729-1983, *IEEE Standard Glossary for Software Engineering Terminology*, 1983 by IEEE, Inc., 345 East 47th Street, NY, NY 10017.

Chapter 5

The inspection process

A N INSPECTION IS a powerful tool that can help achieve significant improvements in software quality. Recent data reported by Capers Jones [1] identified several companies that have managed to achieve defect removal efficiencies exceeding 99%. As mentioned in Chapter 3, the defect removal efficiency is calculated as:

$$\frac{\text{number of defects found prior release of a product}}{\substack{\text{the number found prior release plus the number reported} \\ \text{by customers during the first } n \text{ months of actual use}}}$$

In each of those best-in-class companies, formal inspections are an important factor that helps achieve such high defect removal efficiencies.

Why are formal inspections such an important part of the software development process? Consider the following:

- Requirements are the most common source of problems in the software development process.
- Requirements are written in English, usually by people who have little or no training in writing requirements for software.
- The English language is imprecise, ambiguous, and nondeterministic.
- Software is precise, unambiguous, and deterministic.

Make a photocopy of this page of the book and give it to 10 colleagues. Ask them to follow the directions and answer the question. Provide no further information. Each person should complete this task in 10 minutes working independently.

Directions: Count the number of occurrences of the letter *e* on this page and write your answer in the space provided.

"While inspections will not solve all problems, they are enormously effective. [Inspections] have been demonstrated to improve both quality and productivity by impressive factors. Inspections are not magic and they should not be considered a replacement for testing, but all software organizations should use inspections or similar technical review methods in all major aspects of their work. This includes requirements, design, implementation, test, maintenance, and documentation" [2].

Answer: The letter *e* appears _____ times.

In practice, you will probably get many different answers to what seems a simple, straightforward question. However, the ambiguity of the English language becomes apparent when you ask people how they arrived at their answers. Some may say, "I counted every *e* on the page, even the ones outside the box." Others may say, "I interpreted the instructions to mean count only every *e* in the box." Still others may say, "I counted only every *e* in the quoted text."

Imagine the confusion and misinterpretation when you start talking about complex technical requirements for software!

This chapter introduces the inspection process. Chapter 6 includes a discussion of how the inspection process can be applied to the different deliverables produced during the software development process.

The inspection process is presented through a collection of FAQs. To supplement the answers to the FAQs, an extensive collection of reference material is included in Appendixes A–F.

5.1 Inspection process FAQs

What is an inspection?

An inspection is a formal, rigorous, in-depth technical review designed to identify problems as close to their point of origin as possible. The inspection process was developed by Michael Fagan [3] while he was at IBM in the 1970s. Inspections have not changed much since they were first described by Fagan. What has changed is the realization that this process can have a significant effect on software quality. Numerous studies [4–6] conducted over the past 20 years have documented the economic benefit of inspections on quality.

The objectives of the inspection process are to:

- Find problems at the earliest possible point in the software development process;
- Ensure that agreement is reached on rework that may need to be done;
- Verify that any rework that is done meets predefined criteria.

In addition to those objectives, inspections also:

- Provide data on product quality and process effectiveness;
- Build technical knowledge among team members;
- Increase the effectiveness of software validation testing;
- Raise the standard of excellence for software engineers.

Why is an inspection considered formal?

An inspection is formal because there are defined roles and responsibilities for each participant. There is also a defined process that is followed in the weeks leading up to the inspection meeting, during the meeting itself, and for the follow-up activities after the meeting. Having a formal process ensures that the objectives of the inspection will be met.

Who participates in an inspection?

An inspection typically requires three to six people. Each person is assigned a specific role, and each role has specific responsibilities associated with it. The roles are:

- The *moderator* coordinates the inspection meeting and leads the discussion.
- The *producer* is the person whose work is being inspected.
- The *reader* paraphrases the work being inspected at the inspection meeting.
- The *inspector* inspects the product.
- The *recorder* records the problems and other issues discussed at the inspection meeting.
- The *manager* is the producer's supervisor.

What are the responsibilities of each role?

Well-defined roles and responsibilities are a key attribute of the inspection process. The roles and responsibilities of the moderator, producer, reader, inspector, recorder, and manager are defined in Appendix A.

Throughout the software development process for a given project, people may be asked to fill several different roles. You may play the role of an inspector at one inspection and be the producer for another. As the producer, you receive the benefits of having a talented group of people help you improve the quality of your work. In return, they will expect the same from you.

Who attends the inspection meeting?

Just as important as who participates in inspections is who does not participate. The manager participates in the inspection process but does not attend the inspection meeting. Experience has shown that the inclusion of a manager at an inspection meeting changes the inspection. Regardless of the manager's behavior at the meeting, the focus consciously or unconsciously shifts from the product to the producer. It is for that reason that managers do not attend inspection meetings.

Why is the producer present?

The producer's responsibilities at the inspection meeting are to clarify, not justify. The producer answers questions but does not attempt to explain why—only what and how. The moderator ensures that comments and criticisms are directed at the product, not at the producer.

How are inspections different from walk-throughs?

Inspections are different from walk-throughs in several key areas, as shown in Table 5.1.

Table 5.1   How Inspections Differ From Walk-Throughs

Attribute	Inspection	Walk-Through
Objectives	Finding problems	Finding problems
	Verifying rework	Discussing alternative solutions
	Focusing on whether product as written meets all requirements	Focusing on demonstrating how product meets all requirements
Decision making	All decisions based on consensus of inspection team	All decisions made by producer
Leadership	Trained moderator	Usually the producer
Attendance	Peers; attendance documented	Peers and technical managers; attendance not documented
Presentation of material	Material presented by reader	Material presented by producer
Metrics	Formally required	Optional
Procedures	Formally documented	Informal
Training	Required for all participants	None required

What are the key attributes of the inspection process?

The key attributes of the inspection process are well-defined roles and responsibilities for the inspection team members; a documented inspection process; a collection of product and process metrics; inspecting against "that which came before"; and a supporting infrastructure.

The roles and responsibilities of the inspection team members are listed in Appendix A. An example inspection process is included in Appendix B. The information in Appendixes A through D can be used to develop an inspection process for your organization.

Product and process metrics can be used to improve the inspection process. For example, a Pareto analysis of defect data collected from several code inspections could be used to revise coding standards. (A Pareto analysis helps separate the *vital few from the trivial many*.) Analysis of process metrics (such as how many errors are found versus how many defects are found) can be used to improve the inspection process. The Inspection Problem Report form and the Inspection Summary form shown in Appendix C illustrate the types of metrics that should be collected.

A basic principle of the inspection process is the inspection of a document or code against "that which came before." In other words, when doing a design inspection, the SDD is inspected against the SRS; when doing a code inspection, the code is inspected against the SDD. In addition, any relevant company or project standards (such as coding conventions) should be used during the inspection.

The final key to a successful and effective inspection process is a supporting infrastructure, that is, support from management. Inspection training is required for all people who are to be involved in the process. The training, which can be completed in a few hours, can be based on information contained in the appendixes. Training is necessary to ensure that each participant is aware of his or her role in the inspection and the responsibilities associated with that role.

Because inspection meetings are very different from other types of meetings in which software engineers usually participate, training in how to behave at an inspection is essential. Participants need to learn how to direct their criticism at the product, not the producer. They need to learn the types of questions to ask (such as, "What does this section of code do?") and, more important, what questions *not* to ask ("Why did you do it *that* way?"). For many software engineers, the temptation to roll up their sleeves and get into problem solving is great. That behavior needs to be changed during an inspection. A good idea for a company implementing inspections is to have a few practice inspections to allow people to become familiar with the process and the group dynamics.

In addition to the commitment to training, project managers need to plan for inspections by including them on project schedules. If inspections are not part of the schedule, they are less likely to occur. Last, but not least, managers and supervisors must allow people to participate on inspection teams. That requires time commitments that sometimes will conflict with other priorities.

Who decides what to inspect?

Deciding what to inspect is not easy. Inspections require a considerable time commitment; therefore, selecting what to inspect needs to be done judiciously.

Usually, a producer and the producer's manager decide on the need for an inspection. It is important to note that the producer's manager is involved only in the decision to conduct the inspection, not in the inspection itself. Potential producers should view inspections as positive steps taken to improve product quality and reduce rework.

Developing criteria is a useful way to help decide when inspections are necessary. For example, the following criteria can be used to select code modules for inspection:

- A module performs functions that are critical to the correct operation of the product.
- A module is determined to be relatively more complex than other modules based on objective evaluation with industry-standard complexity metrics (such as the McCabe cyclomatic complexity [7] or Halstead's software science [8]).
- In the past, a relatively high number of errors have been found in modules that perform similar functions.
- The module was written by a relatively new or inexperienced software engineer.

Similar criteria should be developed for each type of product that will be inspected.

How do you know if you are ready to perform an inspection?

Being "ready" to perform an inspection means that the necessary documentation has been prepared and is in order. It also means that the required inspection training has been performed and that there is support from management. Table 5.2 lists the documentation that is required for an inspection.

What materials are required to conduct an inspection?

The materials needed to conduct the inspection are listed in Table 5.2. Many companies have developed their own internal coding standards and conventions. For consistency, improved readability and maintainability, and so on, it is important that such documents be included in code inspections.

Prompting checklists can be used for all types of inspections. The checklists should address common problems observed in the information being inspected and should be updated frequently based on the product and process data collected during inspections. Examples of checklists are included in Appendix D.

Table 5.2   Ready for Inspection?

Type of Inspection	Item Being Inspected	Ready To Inspect If...	Materials Required for Inspection Team
Requirements	SRS	Inspection training has been performed.	SRS and product concept specification (or document that precedes SRS)
		Product concept (or document that precedes SRS) has been reviewed and approved.	Requirements checklist*
		SRS has been approved.	
Design	SDD	Inspection training has been performed.	SDD and the SRS
		SRS has been inspected and all outstanding issues have been resolved.	Design checklist*
		SDD has been approved.	
Code	Source code modules	Inspection training has been performed.	Line-numbered source code listing and the SDD
		The SDD has been inspected and all outstanding issues have been resolved.	Company coding standards
		Modules have been selected for inspection based on defined criteria.*	Coding Checklist*
		The source code has been compiled with no errors.	
Validation tests	Test procedures	Inspection training has been performed.	Test procedures and SRS

Type of Inspection	Item Being Inspected	Ready To Inspect If...	Materials Required for Inspection Team
		The SRS has been inspected and all outstanding issues have been resolved.	(Validation tests are tests against the SRS.)
		Test plan and procedures have been approved.	

* Examples are included in Appendix D.

How are these materials disseminated?

The producer is responsible for providing the required materials to the moderator in a timely manner. The moderator then is responsible for distributing the materials to the inspection team. This can be done at the overview meeting (if one is scheduled). The moderator ensures that the inspection team receives the material at least five working days prior to the inspection meeting.

What if the inspection team does not have five working days to review the materials?

Remember the Boy Scout motto ("Be Prepared")? Well, that should be the motto of the inspection team as well. Experience has shown that five working days is the minimum required for participants to prepare adequately for an inspection. There is no point conducting the inspection if the team is not prepared. If the team is not prepared, the moderator should postpone the inspection meeting.

We are having our first inspection and I am one of the inspectors. What should I do to prepare?

First, know your role and responsibilities (see Appendix A). Next, based on the information you have received, familiarize yourself with the document you are inspecting. Review that document against the "document which came before," using prompting checklists and standards as reminders of things to check. Now go back to the document you are inspecting and look for potential problems: places where requirements defined in the earlier document are not met or places where standards and conventions are not followed.

Each time you find a potential problem, record it on an Inspection Problem Report form (see Appendix C). Continue until you have gone through the entire document. If, during your preparation, you have questions that deal with understanding what is being done (not *why* it is being done), ask the moderator or producer for clarification before the inspection meeting. Keep track of your preparation time.

Keep in mind that your objective is to find problems, not solve them.

Who decides what is a problem?

The inspection team reaches consensus on each issue raised and decides what issues are to be recorded as errors or defects.

What is an error?

An error is a problem in which the software or its documentation does not meet defined requirements and is found *at* the point of origin. For example, a coding problem found during a code inspection is an error.

What is a defect?

A defect is a problem in which the software or its documentation does not meet defined requirements and is found *beyond* the point of origin. For example, a requirements problem found during a code inspection is a defect.

What if the producer doesn't agree?

The producer does not get to vote! Problems recorded as errors or defects are decided by the inspection team. The producer does not participate in making those decisions.

I am an inspector, I have completed my preparation, and it is time for the inspection meeting. What happens now?

A typical inspection meeting proceeds in the following manner.

1. The moderator calls the meeting to order and determines if the inspectors are prepared.

2. If the moderator is satisfied that the team is adequately prepared, the inspection begins. The reader starts by paraphrasing the first chunk of information from the work product.

3. The moderator then goes around the table and solicits any potential errors or defects from the team members. Each potential error or

defect is discussed, and the team reaches consensus as to whether a potential problem should be recorded as an error or a defect.

4. The recorder records each potential problem on an Inspection Problem Report form and ensures that the information is complete and accurate and reflects all team discussion and/or clarification.

5. After the reader has completed paraphrasing the whole work product, the moderator asks the recorder to read back all the problem reports to ensure they were recorded correctly.

6. The team decides if the severity of the problems found warrants another inspection or if the moderator can review the corrective action without another inspection meeting.

7. The recorder records the meeting duration information on the Inspection Summary form.

8. If another meeting is required, the moderator schedules the next meeting. The moderator then adjourns the meeting.

How does the moderator know if the inspectors are prepared?

One way of determining if the team is prepared is to ask each inspector to write down how much time he or she spent preparing for the meeting. If, in the moderator's opinion, the team is not adequately prepared, the moderator postpones the meeting. Alternatively, the moderator can meet with the inspectors before the meeting to see if they are prepared.

How does the moderator keep the meeting focused?

It is not always easy. Selecting an individual to act as moderator is crucial to the success of the inspection. An ineffective moderator can be detrimental to the inspection process. The person selected must have the ability and the skills to keep the meeting focused and to deflect criticism from the producer and onto the product. A good moderator will intervene as little as possible but as much as necessary. Training and practice are key.

What happens if the producer becomes defensive?

The moderator needs to take control and reassure the producer that the comments are directed at the product, not at him or her. The moderator needs to reinforce the objective of the inspection, which is to find—not fix—problems and to remind everyone to stay focused on that objective.

How do you justify the preparation time required for an inspection?

The preparation time is justified by the following:

- Have a large group of inspectors from which to select, so each participant spends only a small amount of time during a given year preparing for an inspection.
- Be selective in what you choose to inspect.
- Document the problems found by the inspection team and compare that effort with the effort required to find the same problems other ways (e.g., through testing).
- Document the amount of time actually spent in an inspection.

Why are inspection meetings limited to two hours? What happens if the meeting runs over?

Inspection meetings require intense concentration and focus. Experience has shown that after two hours the ability of most people to concentrate and remain focused decreases. If the meeting runs over two hours, the moderator schedules a continuation meeting for another day.

What information (if any) should be made public regarding inspections?

This issues is controversial because most people are averse to having what is perceived as their competence (or incompetence, as the case may be) being posted for all to see. Rather than posting results of individual inspections, consider posting only summary results after half a dozen or so inspections have been completed. In that way, people will see that management supports quality improvement without personalizing it. This subject is discussed in more detail in Chapter 6.

When is the inspection officially complete?

The inspection is officially complete when the moderator closes out the rework section on the Inspection Problem Report forms for all problems identified.

5.2   Summary

According to Jones:

> All the best-in-class companies that are pushing or exceeding 99% [defect-removal] efficiency levels use formal inspections, quality assurance groups, and trained testing specialists. Of course, high defect-removal efficiency does not guarantee success. A company can have unhappy or dissatisfied customers for other reasons. However, high levels of customer satisfaction strongly correlate with high levels of defect-removal efficiency. Conversely, software firms whose defect-removal efficiency levels sag below 85% almost never have really happy clients because their software is too unreliable [1].

REFERENCES

[1]. Jones, C., "Software Defect-Removal Efficiency," *IEEE Computer*, Vol. 29, No. 4, April 1996, pp. 94–95.

[2] Humphrey, W. S., *Managing the Software Process*, Reading, MA: Addison-Wesley, 1989, p. 172.

[3] Fagan, M., "Design and Code Inspections To Reduce Errors and Improve Program Development," *IBM Systems Journal*, No. 3, 1976, pp. 182–210.

[4] Humphrey, W. S., *Managing the Software Process*, Reading, MA: Addison-Wesley, 1989, pp. 186–187.

[5] Grady, R. B., and T. Van Slack, "Key Lessons in Achieving Widespread Inspection Use," *IEEE Software*, Vol. 11, 1994, pp. 46–57.

[6] Barnard, J., and A. Price, "Managing Code Inspection Information," *IEEE Software*, Vol. 11, March 1994, pp. 59–69.

[7] McCabe, T. J., "A Software Complexity Measure," *IEEE Trans. Software Engineering*, Vol. 2, 1976.

[8] Halstead, H. M., *Elements of Software Science*, New York: North-Holland, 1977.

Further reading

Boehm, B. W., *Software Engineering Economics*, Englewood Cliffs, NJ: Prentice-Hall, 1981.

Fagan, M. E., "Advances in Software Inspections," *IEEE Trans. Software Engineering*, Vol. SE-12, 1986, pp. 774–751.

Friedman, D. P., and G. M. Weinberg, *Walkthroughs, Inspections, and Technical Reviews*, 3rd Ed., New York: Dorset House, 1990.

Gilb, T., and D. Graham, *Software Inspection*, Wokingham, U.K.: Addison-Wesley, 1993.

Gilb, T., *Principles of Software Engineering Management*, Reading, MA: Addison-Wesley, 1988.

Hatton, L., "Static Inspection: Tapping the Wheels of Software," *IEEE Software*, Vol. 12, 1995, pp. 85–87.

Myers, G. J., *The Art of Software Testing*, New York: Wiley, 1979.

Weinberg, G. M., *The Psychology of Computer Programming*, New York: Van Nostrand Rheinhold, 1971.

Resources on the WWW

At the time of publication, the *Software Inspection and Review Organization* (SIRO) home page could be found at http://www.ics.hawaii.edu/~siro/. SIRO is a voluntary organization devoted to the exchange of information about group-based examination of software work products. The scope of the SIRO includes, but is not restricted to:

- Promoting an exchange of ideas and information on the state of practice;
- Facilitating emerging inspection and review techniques;
- Providing a clearinghouse for support resources;
- Surveying and reporting on industry use of techniques and metrics.

SIRO maintains an extensive bibliography of materials related to inspections, formal technical reviews, and walkthroughs.

Chapter 6

Applying the inspection process

TO BE MOST EFFECTIVE, inspections should be an integral part of the software development process. The inspection process can be easily adapted and applied to a variety of deliverables associated with the software development process, including:

- The SRS;
- The SDD;
- The source code;
- Test procedures.

Before discussing how to adapt and apply the inspection process, we need to review issues related to integrating inspections into the software development process and, more importantly, into a company's culture. The goal here is for inspections to become institutionalized.

6.1 Attributes of a good process

The SEI has conducted an extensive amount of research into issues that affect an organization's ability to consistently develop high-quality software. As would be expected, the software development process is a key element in delivering high-quality software. The SEI has identified the following key attributes of a "good" process:

- The process is written.
- The process is flexible and can be changed.
- Everyone agrees to follow the process.
- The process includes metrics that are used to measure the effectiveness of the process.
- Metrics are the basis for changing the process.
- The process is actively managed.

These attributes, while applicable to almost any process, are particularly relevant for software-related processes and are indicators of process maturity. In a highly competitive global economy, those organizations that exhibit higher levels of process maturity will produce higher quality products and will be more productive, efficient, and profitable.

To help introduce inspections into your organization, an example of an inspection process is included in Appendixes A through F. This material can be used to document your inspection process and form the basis for inspection training materials.

6.1.1 Institutionalizing inspections

Making inspections part of a company's culture can be a difficult task. Management may question the cost savings that can be realized by judicious use of inspections and may ask for an economic justification. As discussed earlier, a lot of economic data are available to justify the use of inspections.

Surprisingly, some software engineers and project managers may be reluctant to accept inspections. Some software engineers fear peer review and have legitimate concerns regarding the use of such reviews as part of performance evaluations. Some project managers may be reluctant to incorporate inspections into project schedules because they do not understand the benefits and tend to focus on short-term objectives (e.g., meeting a schedule) at the expense of long-term goals (e.g., increasing customer satisfaction). Understanding the root causes of this reluctance is essential to overcoming resistance to institutionalizing inspections.

Some key management issues that need to be addressed are:

- Does management understand and support the objectives of the inspection process?
- Is management willing to commit the resources necessary to train inspectors?
- Is management willing to include inspections in project schedules?

Issues related to the software development process include:

- Is there a written software development process? If not, could one be developed?
- Is there management support for a software development process?
- If a software development process exists, can it be modified to include inspections at appropriate points in the process?
- Is the software development process being actively managed?
- Does the software engineering group support the inspection process?
- Are resources available to train people in the inspection process? Is there a commitment to provide training over time as new employees are hired?

Issues pertaining to inspection metrics are:

- Are the product and process metrics that will be collected from inspections defined? How will those data be used?
- Is there a continuous improvement process that would drive improvements to the inspection process based on collected data?

6.1.2   Real-life experiences

Many companies have successfully institutionalized inspections. Hewlett-Packard has used inspections successfully for over 15 years. The results of widespread adoption of the inspection process at Hewlett-Packard were recently reported [1]. From that extensive experience base, Hewlett-Packard has developed a plan to standardize the use of inspections across the company. Key parts of the plan are:

- Proactive support of inspection champions and sponsors;

- Reinforcement of management awareness with economic justification for inspections;
- Building of an infrastructure strong enough to achieve and hold software core competence;
- Measurement of the extent to which the process is used.

Hewlett-Packard's standardization plan is not an attempt to regulate the inspection process but rather to ensure that the process is applied in a manner that is most effective for the organizations using it.

Bell Laboratories (now Lucent Technologies) has been measuring the effectiveness of their formal inspections since 1986 [2]. By applying a set of metrics to over two dozen software projects, the cost of removing defects with code inspections was reduced by 300% when compared with testing alone.

Further information regarding experiences with the inspection process can be found on the WWW on the SIRO home page.

6.2 Requirements inspections

Requirements are frequently subject to misinterpretation. Misinterpretation is usually the result of poorly written, incomplete, inconsistent, and ambiguous requirements. An obvious question is "Why can't we write better requirements?" Unfortunately, there is no simple solution for this problem. Many people with different backgrounds and skill sets typically are involved in the requirements writing process, and most of them are not aware of the impact that poorly written requirements can have on a software development project. There are a couple of things you can do, however, to teach people how to write good requirements.

First, provide an example of a well-written requirements document. If you cannot find one, define some attributes for good requirements documents. Examples of such attributes are included in Appendix E. Second, develop a Requirements Inspection Checklist, similar to the one in Appendix D, that is specific to your organization and its products. The key to making checklists effective is to update them frequently with new information gleaned from inspections performed at your company.

Once you have identified an example of a well-written requirements document, attributes for good requirements, and a Requirements Inspection Checklist, call a meeting with the people who usually write requirements and review the material with them. Let them know that the requirements they write will be measured against these standards. Stress the importance of writing good requirements in terms of the economic impact on the company. Studies have shown that the same error that costs $350 to find and fix in the requirements definition phase of a project can cost more than $12,000 (more than 34 times as much!) to find and fix in the validation testing phase [3].

6.2.1   Objectives of requirements inspections

The objectives of a requirements inspection are to inspect the SRS against the document that preceded it and to answer the following questions:

- Is each requirement in the SRS consistent with and traceable to the document that preceded the SRS?
- Is each requirement in the SRS clear, concise, internally consistent, unambiguous, and, most important, testable?
- Are we building the right product?

6.2.2   Requirements inspection prerequisites

In the planning of a requirements inspection, the following prerequisites should be met:

- Have all inspection team members received inspection process training? (*Note:* This prerequisite applies to *all* types of inspections and, for the sake of brevity, will not be repeated.)
- Has the document that preceded the SRS been reviewed and approved?
- Has the SRS been internally reviewed?
- Is there a Requirements Inspection Checklist? (*Note:* an example of a requirements checklist is included in Appendix D.)
- Once these issues have been addressed, the inspection process can proceed.

6.2.3   The requirements inspection process

6.2.3.1   The planning phase

During the planning phase, the moderator and the inspection team are selected. For a requirements inspection, the moderator should select inspectors from a wide range of disciplines in the organization. For example, the inspection team should include representatives from software engineering, software QA, marketing, customer support, technical publications, manufacturing, and other relevant groups within the organization. Selecting inspectors from several disciplines and functions will result in a much better inspection of the SRS because the product will be inspected from many different points of view.

The moderator and the producer identify relevant inspection materials, including:

- The SRS to be inspected;
- The document that preceded the SRS;
- The Requirements Inspection Checklist (see Appendix D);
- The attributes of good requirements specifications (see Appendix E).

Each member of the inspection team needs to make a commitment to devote the necessary time to the inspection process. In the case of a requirements inspection, preparation time will vary based on familiarity with the product and the product's complexity. As a rule of thumb, preparation time can be estimated at about 10 pages per hour. Of course, that estimate can vary significantly based on many factors. The duration of the inspection meeting should be based on an inspection rate of about 10–20 pages per hour. As the organization gains experience with the inspection process, these estimates can be revised accordingly.

The moderator sets the date, time, and location for the inspection meeting and distributes the inspection materials at least five working days prior to the meeting. The moderator should record the total planning time on the Inspection Summary form.

6.2.3.2 The preparation phase

During the preparation phase, each member of the inspection team prepares for the inspection meeting by reviewing the inspection materials and noting potential discrepancies in the SRS. The requirements checklist should be used to focus attention on specific areas that have been problems previously. Inspectors should record each potential discrepancy on an Inspection Problem Report form (see Appendix C) so that page numbers, questions, and other references can be recorded ahead of time. That will save time during the inspection meeting.

Inspectors are encouraged to ask questions of the producer during the preparation phase. Such questions should be aimed at providing understanding and clarification, not justification.

The members of the inspection team should keep track of their preparation time. The moderator records the total preparation time of the team on the Inspection Summary form.

6.2.3.3   The inspection meeting phase

At the inspection meeting, the moderator must first determine if the inspection team is adequately prepared. One way to do that is to ask each member of the team to write down how much time he or she spent in preparation. Another way to judge preparedness is to ask to see the Inspection Problem Report forms. A third way is for the moderator to meet with the inspectors individually before the meeting to assess preparedness. The moderator uses his or her best judgment to decide if the team is prepared. The moderator has to be willing (and able) to postpone the inspection meeting if, in the moderator's judgment, the team is not adequately prepared. By taking such action, the moderator reinforces the need for preparation.

If the team is prepared, the moderator begins the inspection by reviewing the ground rules (outlined in Appendix B). The moderator then goes around the table and asks for potential discrepancies on a paragraph-by-paragraph basis.

Each potential discrepancy is discussed. As the team reaches consensus on each potential discrepancy, it is so noted on the Inspection Problem Report form. After all potential discrepancies have been discussed, the moderator recaps and asks the team if they feel a follow-up inspection is warranted. If not, the moderator will work with the producer to ensure that corrective action is completed.

The moderator records the duration of the meeting and completes the Inspection Summary form (refer to Appendix C). Two working days after the meeting, the moderator distributes meeting minutes.

6.2.3.4   The follow-up phase

The moderator works with the producer to resolve discrepancies raised at the meeting. On successful completion, the moderator completes the Corrective Action portion of the Inspection Summary form to indicate that the inspection has been completed.

6.2.4   Process and product improvements

Product improvements that can be expected as a result of performing requirements inspections are that costly requirements errors can be detected and removed early in the software development process.

The process improvements that can result from requirements inspections include the following:

- Inspections are a detection cost. Their cost needs to be compared to the cost of correcting problems that would have not been detected had the inspections not been performed.
- After several inspections, the information on the types of discrepancies being found can be assessed and any trends identified. If similar types of discrepancies are being found, consider adding additional items to the Requirements Checklist to help prevent those discrepancies from occurring in the future.

6.3 Design inspection

Finally, there are those systems in which the design errors prove so gross that no system test is ever reached—the system collapses of its own developmental weight before integration is achieved. How many of these does it take to justify the institution of design reviews?

D. P. Friedman and G. M. Weinberg,
Walkthroughs, Inspections, and Technical Reviews, 3rd Ed.,
New York: Dorset House, 1990, p. 310

Almost every software engineer can relate to Friedman and Weinberg's observation. Unfortunately, we continue to deceive ourselves into believing that we are capable of designing very complex systems without the benefit of design inspections. More often than not, such projects are not successful, and organizations spend enormous sums of money correcting problems that never should have occurred in the first place. In a business climate that is constantly looking for cost savings and improved productivity, this is one activity that could result in significant savings, if only it were applied.

6.3.1 Objectives of the design inspection

A design inspection should help answer the following questions:

- Does the design, as expressed in the SDD, address all the requirements of the SRS?

- Are all design elements traceable to specific requirements contained in the SRS?
- Are we building the right product?
- Does the design conform to project and company standards?

6.3.2 Design inspection prerequisites

in the planning of a design inspection, the following prerequisites should be met:

- Has the SRS been inspected and all follow-up actions completed?
- Has the SDD been internally reviewed?
- Is there a Design Inspection Checklist? (*Note:* Examples of a High-Level Design Checklist and a Detailed Design Checklist are included in Appendix D.)
- If the design is done using CASE tools, are relevant reports and diagrams (data dictionaries, data flow diagrams, entity-relationship diagrams, etc.) from such tools available?

Once these issues have been addressed, the inspection process can proceed.

6.3.3 The design inspection process

Design inspections should be performed on those aspects of the product design that warrant an inspection. How do you decide what warrants an inspection? You need to use good engineering judgment. Every aspect of the design cannot be inspected, so you need to be selective in what you inspect. Those aspects of the design that are new, that have been troublesome in the past, that are crucial to the proper functioning of the product are all appropriate criteria to use in deciding what to inspect.

In addition, software design is sometimes done in two stages: high-level design and detailed design. If that is the case in your company, it should be taken into account in the planning of the design inspection.

6.3.3.1 The planning phase

During the planning phase, the moderator and the producer select the inspection team. Given the nature of the SDD, inspection team members should be selected from software engineering, software QA, and other functions as appropriate. For example, if the design being inspected is for software that interfaces to some hardware the company develops, include an engineer from the hardware group on the inspection team.

Again, the moderator needs to get commitment from inspection team members that they can take the time needed to prepare for the inspection meeting. A design inspection may require more preparation time than a requirements inspection because the information is more complex and abstract. As a rule of thumb, preparation time for a design inspection should be based on about five pages per hour. The inspection meeting should be based on an inspection rate of about 5–10 pages per hour.

The moderator and the producer together decide if an optional overview meeting is needed based on the following factors:

- The inspection team's familiarity with the product;
- The complexity of the SDD;
- The amount and the complexity of the inspection materials.

If an overview meeting is needed, the moderator and the producer determine what material to present at the overview meeting. The producer is responsible for presenting the information, while the moderator arranges to distribute the inspection materials at the overview meeting.

The moderator sets the date, time, and location for the overview meeting (if one is needed) and the inspection meeting and distributes the inspection materials at least five working days prior to the inspection meeting. If an overview meeting is held, the moderator distributes the inspection materials at that time.

The moderator records the total planning time and time spent on an overview meeting on the Inspection Summary form.

6.3.3.2 The overview meeting phase

The purpose of the overview meeting is to familiarize the inspection team with the product and the inspection materials to facilitate understanding. At the overview meeting, the producer presents an overview of the product, in an attempt to show how the piece fits into the big picture. The producer should also review the organization and the content of the inspection materials so the team becomes familiar with what is included.

Inspection team members can ask questions at the overview meeting as long as the goal is gaining an understanding of the material being presented. The moderator ensures that questions from the team are along those lines.

The moderator records the time spent preparing for the overview meeting as well as the total time spent by the team at the overview meeting on the Inspection Summary form

6.3.3.3   The preparation phase

During the preparation phase for a design inspection, team members should become very familiar with the inspection materials, the SDD, and the appropriate Design Checklist (high-level design or detailed design). The Design Checklist (examples are included in Appendix D) is used to focus the inspectors' attention on those areas that are known problem areas.

The inspection team member who is acting as the reader should, in addition to preparing as an inspector, be able to paraphrase sections, or chunks, of the design document so the moderator can focus the team's attention on one chunk at a time.

Each inspector should record any discrepancies on a Inspection Problem Report form and keep track of his or her preparation time. The moderator records the total preparation time on the Inspection Summary form.

6.3.3.4   The inspection meeting phase

At the inspection meeting, the moderator first determines if the inspection team is adequately prepared and reviews the ground rules described in Appendix B.

The moderator begins the inspection by asking the reader to paraphrase the first chunk from the SDD. The moderator then asks the team for potential discrepancies in that chunk. Comments on another part of the SDD are not voiced until the reader gets to that chunk.

The team must reach consensus on each potential discrepancy and also decide how to categorize each discrepancy they do agree on. The information is recorded on the Inspection Problem Report form and is used later as the basis for making improvements to the Design Checklist.

After all the chunks have been discussed, the moderator recaps the discrepancies the team has agreed on and asks if the team wants to schedule a follow-up inspection. If it is agreed that a follow-up inspection is not warranted, the moderator is responsible for working with the producer and reviewing the corrective actions. If the team wants a follow-up inspection, the moderator schedules it.

The moderator records the duration of the inspection meeting on the Inspection Summary form and adjourns the meeting. The moderator distributes meeting minutes within two working days of the meeting.

6.3.3.5 The follow-up phase

As requested by the team, the moderator works with the producer to resolve discrepancies raised at the meeting. On successful completion, the moderator completes the Corrective Action portion of the Inspection Summary form to indicate that the inspection has been completed.

6.3.4   Product and process improvements

The following benefits to product improvement can be expected as a result of performing design inspections:

- Design inspections help ensure that important design decisions are not postponed to the coding phase. By making decisions earlier, you reduce the risk of making the wrong decisions later, thus reducing the number of potential coding errors.

- Design inspections help improve maintainability by ensuring that design information is accurate and documented.

Process improvements that can be expected as a result of design inspections include:

- Data collected from inspections can be used to measure the cost of quality.

- Improvements to Design Inspection Checklists can be made based on a review of the types of discrepancies found in several inspections.

6.4 Code inspection

We didn't mean to, but in software we have created the first artifact that exhibits the human duality of body and soul. The soul of software is invisible, intangible, silent, weightless, deaf, mute, blind, paralyzed. Like a soul, too, it is complex and hard to understand. It is a structure of logical symbols organized in a framework according to someone's model of some aspect of the world. How do you visualize the invisible? How do you grasp the intangible? How do you hear the silent?

L. R. Weiner,
Digital Woes: Why We Should Not Depend on Software,
Reading, MA: Addison-Wesley, 1993, p. 38

Most software engineers have at least one story of a bug that they introduced into some product that probably would have been caught if the code had been inspected. The cost of finding and fixing one bug can range from 10 to 100 times the cost of finding and fixing the bug at a code inspection. That is why code inspections should become part of the software development process.

6.4.1 Objectives of the code inspection

A code inspection should help answer the following questions:

- Is the code is consistent with the design as expressed in the SDD?
- Is the code traceable to specific requirements identified in the SDD?
- Are we building the right product?
- Does the code conforms to all project and company standards?

6.4.2 Code inspection prerequisites

In the planning of a code inspection, the following prerequisites should be met:

- Has the SDD been inspected and all follow-up actions completed?
- Has the code been compiled with no errors? Has a tool like Lint been used to identify other potential coding errors?
- Is there a Code Inspection Checklist? (*Note:* Examples of checklists for C and C++ are included in Appendix D.)

Once those issues have been addressed, the inspection process proceeds.

6.4.3 The code inspection process

Code inspections are the most frequently used type of inspection. That is probably due to the fact that we tend to focus a lot of attention on the coding phase of the software development process to the detriment of earlier phases.

A key aspect of code inspections is deciding what to inspect. Code inspections require much more preparation and concentration than do requirements inspections and even design inspections. Therefore, judiciously choosing what to inspect is important to maximize the benefit. An organization should develop criteria similar to those shown in Appendix F to help make that decision.

6.4.3.1 The planning phase

The moderator and the producer jointly recruit the members of the inspection team. Team members should be selected based on their expertise in software engineering, their familiarity with the product, and their involvement with the project. People from groups other than software engineering (user interface, software QA, hardware engineering, etc.) should be considered if they are able to understand and evaluate the material being inspected (i.e., they have at least reading knowledge of the language in which the software is written).

Again, the moderator needs to get commitment from inspection team members that they can take the time needed to prepare for the inspection. A code inspection will require more preparation time than a design inspection because the information is more complex and abstract. As a rule of thumb, preparation time should be based on about 50 lines of C source code per hour. The inspection meeting should be based on an inspection rate of about 100–200 lines of C source code per hour. (*Note:* A line of C source code is not a well-defined entity.)

The moderator and the producer together decide if an optional overview meeting is needed based on the following:

- The inspection team's familiarity with the product;
- The complexity of the module being inspected;
- The complexity of the inspection materials.

If an overview meeting is needed, the moderator and producer determine what material to present at the overview meeting. The producer is responsible for presenting the information, while the moderator arranges to distribute the inspection materials at the overview meeting.

The inspection materials should include the SDD (the document that precedes the code), a line-numbered source listing of the code (to facilitate references to specific lines of code), and a Coding Checklist (similar to that included in Appendix D).

The moderator sets the date, time, and location for the overview meeting (if one is needed) and the inspection meeting and distributes the inspection materials at least five working days prior to the inspection meeting. If an overview meeting is held, the moderator distributes the inspection materials at that time.

The moderator records the inspectors' total planning time and time spent at the overview meeting on the Inspection Summary form.

6.4.3.2 The overview meeting phase

The purpose of the overview meeting is to familiarize the inspection team with the product and the inspection materials. At the meeting, the producer presents an overview of the product, in an attempt to show how the module fits into the big picture. The producer also reviews the organization and the content of the inspection materials so the team becomes familiar with what is included.

Inspection team members are free to ask questions at the overview meeting as long as the questions are aimed at gaining an understanding of the material being presented. The moderator ensures that questions from the team are kept along those lines.

6.4.3.3 The preparation phase

To prepare for the inspection meeting, each inspector becomes very familiar with the module being inspected, the SDD, and the Coding Checklist. Each inspector reviews the module's source listing and looks for potential discrepancies between the code and the SDD. The Coding Checklist helps inspectors focus attention on areas known to be problems. Each discrepancy is noted on an inspection Problem Report form, identifying the relevant line numbers in the source listing and SDD paragraph references.

In addition to his or her inspection role, the reader must also be able to paraphrase sections or chunks of the source code so the moderator can focus the team's attention on one chunk at a time.

6.4.3.4 The inspection meeting phase

At the inspection meeting, the moderator must first determine if the inspection team is adequately prepared and reviews the ground rules as described in Appendix B.

The moderator begins the inspection by asking the reader to paraphrase the first chunk from the module source listing. The reader does so, and the moderator then asks the team for potential discrepancies on that chunk. Comments on another part of the code are not voiced until the reader gets to that chunk.

The team must reach consensus on each potential discrepancy and also decide how to categorize each discrepancy. This information is recorded on the Inspection Problem Report form and is used later as the basis for making improvements to the Coding Checklist.

After all the chunks have been discussed, the moderator recaps the discrepancies on which the team has agreed and asks if the team wants to schedule a follow-up inspection. If the team decides that a follow-up inspection is not warranted, the moderator is responsible for working with the producer and reviewing corrective actions. If the team wants a follow-up inspection, the moderator schedules it.

The moderator records the duration of the inspection meeting on the Inspection Summary form and adjourns the meeting. The moderator distributes meeting minutes within two working days of the meeting.

6.4.3.5 The follow-up phase

As requested by the team, the moderator works with the producer to resolve discrepancies raised at the meeting. On successful completion, the moderator completes the Corrective Action portion of the Inspection Summary form to indicate that the inspection has been completed.

6.4.4 Product and process improvements

The following product improvements can be expected as a result of a code inspection:

- Code inspections will help ensure that the code correctly implements the SDD. That means fewer bugs will be found during testing, thus shortening the overall testing phase.

- Code inspections will help improve maintainability by ensuring that design information is accurate and documented and also will result in more people becoming knowledgeable with the code.

Process improvements that can be expected to result from code inspections include:

- Data collected from inspections can be used to measure the cost of quality.

- Improvements to Code Inspection Checklists can be made based on a review of the types of discrepancies found from several code inspections.

6.5 Test procedure inspection

Like all other deliverables produced during the software development process, tests are subject to misunderstanding and can benefit from selective inspection. The primary benefit to be gained by application of the inspection process to test procedures is that it can help identify potential misunderstandings between the software engineers and the software validation test engineers. Identifying and correcting such misunderstandings before the validation testing phase begins results in a more effective and efficient testing process.

6.5.1   Objectives of the test procedure inspection

Test inspections should answer the following questions:

- Do the validation tests accurately reflect requirements defined in the SRS?
- Have validation tests taken advantage of knowledge of the design where appropriate?
- Is the project ready to enter the validation testing phase?

6.5.2   Test procedure inspection prerequisites

In the planning of a code inspection, the following prerequisites should be met:

- Have the tests been reviewed internally and executed at least once?
- Is there a Test Procedure Inspection Checklist? (*Note:* An example is included in Appendix D.)

Once these issues have been addressed, the inspection process can proceed.

6.5.3   The test procedure inspection process

6.5.3.1   The planning phase

The moderator and the producer should jointly recruit the members of the inspection team. Team members should be selected based on their expertise in software engineering, their familiarity with product requirements, and their involvement with the features that are being tested. In most cases, an overview meeting is not required.

The moderator and the producer identify relevant inspection materials, including:

- The SRS;
- The test procedures to be inspected;
- The Test Procedure Inspection Checklist (see Appendix D).

As for all inspections, commitment from the team members is essential.

The moderator sets the date, time, and location for the inspection meeting and distributes the inspection materials at least five working days prior to the meeting. The moderator should record the total planning time on the Inspection Summary form.

6.5.3.2 The preparation phase

To prepare for the inspection meeting, each inspector becomes very familiar with the test procedures being inspected, the SRS, and the Test Procedure Inspection Checklist. Each inspector reviews the test procedures and looks for potential discrepancies between the test and the SRS. The checklist helps focus attention on areas known to be problems. Each discrepancy is noted on an Inspection Problem Report form, identifying the relevant locations in the test procedure and SRS paragraph references.

In addition his or her preparation as an inspector, the reader also must be able to paraphrase chunks of the test procedure so the moderator can focus the team's attention on one chunk at a time.

6.5.3.3 The inspection meeting phase

At the inspection meeting, the moderator first determines if the inspection team is adequately prepared and reviews the ground rules as described in Appendix B.

The moderator begins the inspection by asking the reader to paraphrase the first chunk from the first test procedure. The reader does so, then moderator asks the team for potential discrepancies on that chunk. Comments on other parts of the test are not voiced until the reader gets to that chunk.

The team must reach consensus on each potential discrepancy and decide how to categorize each discrepancy. This information is recorded on the Inspection Problem Report form and is used later as the basis for making improvements to the Test Procedure Inspection Checklist.

After all the chunks have been discussed, the moderator recaps the discrepancies on which the team has agreed and asks if the team wants to schedule a follow-up inspection. If the team decides that a follow-up is not warranted, the moderator is responsible for working with the producer and reviewing the corrective actions. If the team wants a follow-up inspection, the moderator schedules it.

The moderator records the duration of the inspection meeting on the Inspection Summary form and adjourns the meeting. The moderator distributes meeting minutes within two working days of the meeting.

6.5.3.4 The follow-up phase

As requested by the team, the moderator works with the producer to resolve discrepancies raised at the meeting. On successful completion, the moderator completes the Corrective Action portion of the Inspection Summary form to indicate that the inspection has been completed.

6.5.4   Product and process improvements

As a result of test procedure inspections, product improvement in the form of reduced testing time can be expected. Test procedure inspections will help ensure that the tests correctly implement the SRS. Because both the code and the test procedures are written based on the SRS, this inspection will help ensure that the tests are an accurate reflection of the SRS.

Process improvements that can be expected to result from test procedure inspections include:

- Data collected from inspections can be used to measure the cost of quality.
- Improvements to the Test Procedure Inspection Checklists can be made based on a review of the types of discrepancies found during several inspections.

6.6   Summary

This chapter discussed how to apply the same inspection process to several different deliverables produced as part of the software development process. Through application of the inspection process and collection of data resulting from inspections, significant improvements can be achieved in both the product and the process.

REFERENCES

[1]   Grady, R. B., and T. VanSlack, "Key Lessons in Achieving Widespread Inspection Use," *IEEE Software*, Vol. 11, 1994, pp. 46–57.

[2]   Barnard, J., and A. Price, "Managing Code Inspection Information," *IEEE Software*, Vol. 11, March 1994, pp. 59–69.

[3]   Good, D. L., "Cost-Effectiveness," *ACM Software Engineering Notes*, Vol. 11, 1986, p. 82.

Chapter 7

Software quality metrics

When you can measure what you are speaking about, and express it in numbers, you know something about it; but when you cannot measure it, when you cannot express it in numbers, your knowledge is of a meager and unsatisfactory kind; it may be the beginning of knowledge, but you have scarcely in your thoughts advanced to the stage of science.

Lord Kelvin, quoted in R. B. Grady and D. L. Caswell,
Software Metrics: Establishing a Company-Wide Program,
Englewood-Cliffs, NJ: Prentice-Hall, 1987

Loosely translated, Lord Kelvin was saying:

"To measure is to know."

Recall the last product your organization released. See if you can answer the following questions about that product:

- How large was the product (as measured by lines of source code or megabytes of memory)?
- What was the overall productivity of the software engineering group on the product (as measured by thousand-lines of code, or KLOC per person-hour)?
- How many bugs were found in the product before it was released?
- How many bugs were found by customers in the first three months after its release?
- Was the overall quality of the product better or worse than the previously released product?

For many software organizations, such basic information is not known. In other industries, this type of information is routinely collected and used by management to make decisions that drive process improvement. In the software industry, however, relatively few organizations routinely collect and use such information to improve the software development process.

Size, productivity, number of defects, and relative quality are key indicators that are extremely important for any organization that is serious about quality improvement.

This chapter examines a process for identifying and collecting software metrics that support software quality and software V&V activities. Chapter 10 discusses some metrics specific to software validation activities. Identifying and collecting software process and product metrics are important in three areas:

- As the software product is being developed, the developers can objectively assess whether the software quality requirements are being met.
- The metrics can provide a quantitative assessment of software quality that can be the basis for decisions regarding the software's fitness for use.
- The company can objectively assess the effectiveness of its software development process.

Several excellent books and articles have been written on software metrics. One of the best was written by Robert Grady and Deborah Caswell [1] and describes their experiences in implementing a companywide software metrics program at Hewlett-Packard.

Another excellent resource for guidance to establishing a software metrics program is the *IEEE Standard for a Software Quality Metrics Methodology* [2]. In addition to defining a framework for identifying and collecting software quality metrics, the standard provides numerous examples and an exhaustive annotated bibliography.

In this chapter, these two sources will be used to present a process for implementing a software metrics program. The purpose of the software metrics program is to identify both process and product metrics. Additionally, specific metrics related to software V&V activities will also be discussed.

7.1 A strategy for implementing a software metrics program

The motivation for a software metrics program comes from the fact that the more attributes of software we can measure, the more control we can exert over changing those attributes in a way that will result in process improvement.

Grady and Caswell's experience in implementing a software metrics program at Hewlett-Packard has resulted in valuable information that an organization can use to start a software metrics program. Grady and Caswell have identified 10 steps that will lead to implementation of a software metrics program. These steps are summarized in Table 7.1 [1].

Table 7.1 Steps for Implementing a Software Metrics Program

1	Define the objectives for the software metrics program.
2	Assign responsibility.
3	Do research.
4	Define the initial metrics to be collected.
5	Sell the initial collection of those metrics.
6	Get tools for automatic data collection and analysis.
7	Establish training in software metrics.
8	Publicize success stories.
9	Create a metrics database.
10	Establish an orderly way for improving the process.

Defining the objectives of a software metrics program are crucial for its success. The objectives should address the expected costs, the cost savings that are possible, and the expected improvements in quality. Remember that quality improvements have both a cost and a cost savings. The costs are associated with the identifying and collecting of the metrics. The cost savings derive from lower support costs after product release, fewer maintenance releases, higher customer satisfaction, and, as a result, increased sales.

Another key lesson we should learn from Grady and Caswell is that the metrics program should be "...only a part of an overall strategy for software development process improvement" [1]. Without an overall program for process improvement, metrics are of little value.

7.2 Software quality metrics framework

IEEE Standard 1061-1992 [2] addresses steps 3, 4, and 6 of Hewlett-Packard's 10-step process and provides a process for answering the two most difficult questions that an organization must address when considering a software metrics program: "What to measure?" and "How to measure it?"

Grady and Caswell suggest starting with three simple metrics: size, defects, and effort. While these three metrics are a good starting place, IEEE Standard 1061-1992 [2] defines an approach, in the form of a plan, for identifying and collecting those metrics that relate to quality requirements.

7.2.1 Definitions

IEEE Standard 1061-1992 [2] defines a methodology for establishing a software quality metrics framework. The standard includes many definitions, a few of which are repeated in Table 7.2.

Table 7.2 Definitions from IEEE Std 1061-1992

Metrics framework:	A tool used for organizing, selecting, communicating, and evaluating the required quality attributes for a software system. A hierarchical breakdown of *factors*, *subfactors*, and *metrics* for a software system.
Quality factor:	A management-oriented attribute of software that contributes to its quality.
Quality subfactor:	A decomposition of a *quality factor* to its technical components.

Direct metric:	A metric applied during development or operations that represents a software *quality factor*.
Predictive metric:	A metric applied during development and used to predict the values of a software *quality factor*.
Software quality metric:	A function whose inputs are software data and whose output is a single numerical value that can be interpreted as the degree to which software possesses a given attribute that affects its quality.
Process metric:	A metric used to measure characteristics of the methods, techniques, and tools employed in developing, implementing, and maintaining the software system.
Product metric:	A metric used to measure that characteristics of documentation and code.

Source: [2]. © 1993 IEEE.

7.2.2   The framework

The software quality metrics framework is shown in Figure 7.1. The framework is a hierarchy that consists of four levels. At the topmost level are the quality requirements that the software product must meet. These requirements usually are expressed in the customer's terms, for example:

- "The product will work on the platforms and operating systems currently used in our organization."

- "The product will be reliable and will provide mechanisms to prevent loss of data."

- "The product will provide the necessary functionality required to accomplish x, y, or z."

- "The product will be easy for our people to use."

The second level of the framework represents specific quality factors that relate to the overall quality requirements. Quality factors are an interpretation of the customer's quality requirements and are shown in Table 7.3. (A complete list of quality factors are included in Appendix A of IEEE Standard 1061.)

The third level of the framework represents quality subfactors that are obtained by decomposing each quality factor into measurable attributes. Quality subfactors are expressed in terms meaningful to software engineers and are independent of any one quality factor. Quality subfactors associated with the quality factors listed in Table 7.3 are shown in Table 7.4. (A complete list of quality subfactors are included in Appendix A of IEEE Standard 1061.)

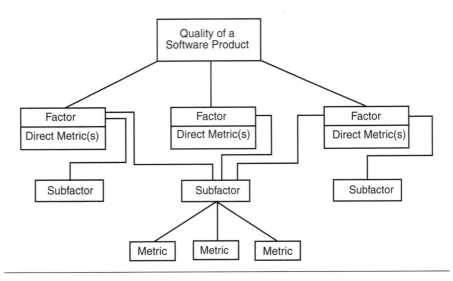

Figure 7.1   Software quality metrics framework. (*Source:* [2]. © 1992 IEEE.)

Table 7.3   Quality Factors Associated With Quality Requirements

Quality Requirement	Quality Factor	Description
The product will work on multiple platforms and operating systems currently being used in our organization.	Portability	An attribute that bears on the ability of software to be transferred from one environment to another.
The product will be reliable and will provide mechanisms to prevent loss of data.	Reliability	An attribute that bears on the capability of software to maintain its level of performance under stated conditions for a stated period of time.
The product will provide the necessary functionality required to accomplish some task description.	Functionality	An attribute that bears on the existence of certain properties and functions that satisfy stated or implied needs of users.
The product will be easy to use.	Usability	An attribute that bears on the effort needed for use (including preparation for use and evaluation of results) and on the individual assessment of such use by users.

Adapted from: [2]. © 1993 IEEE.

Table 7.4 Quality Subfactors Associated With Quality Factors

Quality Factor	Quality Subfactors	Description
Portability	Hardware independence	The degree to which software does not depend on specific hardware environments
	Software independence	The degree to which the software does not depend on specific software environments
	Installability	The effort required to adjust software to a new environment
	Reusability	The degree to which software can be reused in applications other than the original application
Reliability	Nondeficiency	The degree to which software does not contain undetected errors
	Error tolerance	The degree to which software will continue to work without a system failure that would cause damage to users; also the degree to which software includes degraded operation and recovery functions
	Availability	The degree to which software remains operable in the presence of system failures
Functionality	Completeness	The degree to which software possesses necessary and sufficient functions to satisfy user needs
	Correctness	The degree to which all software functions are specified
	Security	The degree to which software can detect and prevent information leak, information loss, illegal use, and system resource destruction

Table 7.4 (Continued)

Quality Factor	Quality Subfactors	Description
	Compatibility	The degree to which new software can be installed without changing environments and conditions that were prepared for the replaced software
	Interoperability	The degree to which software can be connected easily with other systems and operated
Usability	Understandability	The amount of effort required to understand software.
	Ease of learning	The degree to which user effort required to understand software is minimized
	Operability	The degree to which the operation of software matches the purpose, environment, and physiological characteristics of users, including ergonomic factors such as color, shape, and sound
	Communicativeness	The degree to which software is designed in accordance with the psychological characteristics of users

Adapted from: [2]. © 1993 IEEE.

At the fourth level are direct metrics. At least one direct metric is associated with each quality factor. Direct metrics serve as the quantitative representation of a quality factor. Examples of direct metrics are shown in Table 7.5.

Table 7.5   Examples of Direct Metrics

Quality Subfactors	Direct Metrics	Description
Hardware independence	Hardware dependencies	Count of hardware dependencies

Quality Subfactors	Direct Metrics	Description
Software independence	Software dependencies	Count of software dependencies
Installability	Installation time	Measure of installation time
Reusability	Other applications software can be used in	Count of number of other applications software can be or has been used in
Nondeficiency	Test coverage	Measure of test coverage
	Inspection coverage	Count of modules that have had code inspection
Error tolerance	Data integrity	Count of situations where user data become corrupted
	Data recovery	Measure of ability to recover corrupted data
Availability	Percentage of time software is available for use	Time software available for use divided by total time software could be available for use (expressed as a percentage)
Completeness	Test coverage	Call pair measure or branch coverage measure
Correctness	Defect density	Count of defects discovered in each version of software prior to release
Security	Data integrity	Count of situations where user data become corrupted
	User security	Number of illegal users who are not prevented from using software.
Compatibility	Environmental changes	Number of environmental variables that must be changed after software is installed
Interoperability	Operability in mixed application environments	Number of mixed application environments software can work in correctly
Understandability	Learning time	Time for new user to learn software features

Table 7.5 (Continued)

Quality Subfactors	Direct Metrics	Description
Ease of learning	Learning time	Time for new user to learn how to perform basic functions of software
Operability	Human factors	Number of negative comments from new users regarding ergonomics
Communicativeness	Human factors	Number of negative comments from new users regarding ergonomics

Adapted from: [2]. © 1993 IEEE.

If we put all the information on quality requirements, quality factors, subfactors and direct metrics together, we have the information shown in Table 7.6.

Table 7.6   Quality Requirements, Quality Factors, Subfactors, and Direct Metrics

Quality Requirement	Quality Factor	Quality Subfactors	Direct Metrics
The product will work on multiple platforms and operating systems currently being used in our organization.	Portability	Hardware independence	Hardware dependencies
		Software independence	Software dependencies
		Installability	Installation time
		Reusability	Other applications software can be used in

Quality Requirement	Quality Factor	Quality Subfactors	Direct Metrics
The product will be reliable and will provide mechanisms to prevent loss of data.	Reliability	Nondeficiency	Test coverage Inspection coverage
		Error tolerance	Data integrity Data recovery
		Availability	Percentage of time software is available for use
The product will provide the necessary functionality required to accomplish some task description.	Functionality	Completeness	Test coverage
		Correctness	Defect density
		Security	Data integrity User security
		Compatibility	Environmental changes
		Interoperability	Operability in mixed application environments
The product will be easy to use.	Usability	Understandability	Learning time
		Ease of learning	Learning time
		Operability	Human factors
		Communicativeness	Human factors

Adapted from: [2]. © 1993 IEEE.

7.2.3   Applying the software quality metrics methodology

This part of the IEEE Software Metrics Methodology answers the "What to measure?" question and can be implemented using a five-step process [2]:

1.   Establish quality requirements.

2. Identify one or more direct metrics associated with each quality requirement.

3. Implement the direct metrics.

4. Analyze the results.

5. Validate the metrics.

7.2.3.1 Establish quality requirements

By far, the most difficult part of this process is establishing quality requirements. There are some hurdles that need to be overcome before the process of identifying quality requirements can begin in earnest. Typically, these hurdles are:

- What group is empowered to define quality requirements?
- How should customers provide input?
- How are requirements conflicts resolved?

First a team must be empowered to define quality requirements. Forming a team that represents all points of view and is acknowledged as the group that will determine quality requirements is essential for success.

Getting customer input can also be tricky. Customers more often tell you what they do *not* want rather than what they *do* want. For example, customers might make statements such as the following.

- "I don't want the software to cause my system to lock up as frequently as the current system does."
- "I don't like they way the user interface works on this application."
- "I don't mind if the system crashes once in a while, as long as I don't lose any data."

Customers are sophisticated when it comes to software products. Customers realize that they cannot afford nor are willing to wait for defect-free software.

So how do you define quality requirements that are representative of what customers expect? First, talk to your customers. Conduct a quality survey or a focus group. Gather information about the quality of your current products. Find out how good competitors products are relative to yours. Do some side-by-side comparisons. And try to put yourself in your customers' shoes. Ask what you would expect if you were buying your products. Survey people in functional groups within the organization who typically deal with customers (such as technical support personnel, field application engineers, and sales reps) and get input on what customers tell them about your products.

Next, you need to associate each quality requirement with a quality factor. (Refer to Appendix A of IEEE Standard 1061.) This step requires an understanding of what the quality requirements are and what the quality factors represent.

Once the association has been completed, the quality factors must be ranked in order of importance. It is at that time that the team must assess technical feasibility, resolve requirement conflicts, and establish priorities. This may take a bit of negotiating and compromising, because some quality requirements will affect costs, schedules, and functionality. Once you have identified the set of quality factors, you need to get buy-in from the rest of the organization.

7.2.3.2 Identify direct metrics

One or more direct metrics are associated with each quality factor. Remember that direct metrics are quantitative measures that reflect the quality factors with which they are associated. Each direct metric is assigned a target value. In that way, we can measure the degree to which the product possesses the attributes associated with the quality factors.

For example, if one of the quality factors selected was usability, a direct metric that could be associated with that factor might be the time it takes for an untrained user to learn how to use the software and perform some specific task. The target value for this metric might be 10 minutes. The set of direct metrics and their target values should be reviewed and approved as well.

Each direct metric selected should be documented. IEEE Standard 1061-1992 [2] suggests a format similar to that summarized in Table 7.7.

Table 7.7   Documenting Direct Metrics

Item	Description
Name	Name of the metric
Impact	Can this metric indicate deficient software quality?
Target value	Numerical value to be achieve to meet quality requirement
Tools	Software/hardware tools required to help compute metric value
Application	Description of how metric result is to be used
Data items	Data required as input to compute metric value
Computation	Steps required to compute metric

Adapted from: [2]. © 1993 IEEE.

Table 7.8 shows an example of how a direct metric might be documented.

Table 7.8   Sample Documentation of a Direct Metric

Item	Description
Name	Number of defects detected in selected modules
Impact	Can impact software quality requirements
Target value	<5
Tools	Spreadsheet
Application	Metric is used for relative comparison to values obtained for other modules
Data items	Count defects detected at code inspections
Computation	Sum number of defects reported against specific modules

Adapted from: [2]. © 1993 IEEE.

7.2.3.3   Implement the direct metrics

The third step of the five-step process is to implement the direct metrics by defining the data collection procedures and associated tools to collect the data needed for the metrics. Each data item required to compute a direct metric should be documented. IEEE Standard 1061-1992 [2] suggests a format for documenting data items, which is summarized in Table 7.9.

Table 7.9   Documenting Data Items Required for Direct Metrics

Item	Description
Name	Name given to a data item
Metrics	Metrics associated with the data item
Definition	Straightforward description of the data item
Source	Location of where the data originate
Procedure	Procedure for collecting the data
Representation	Manner in which data are represented; e.g. its precision, format, units
Storage	Location where the data are stored

Adapted from: [2]. © 1993 IEEE.

7.2.3.4   Analyze software quality metric results

Once the data collection is underway, the results need to be analyzed within the context of the project's overall software quality requirements. Any metrics that fall outside their respective targets should be identified for further analysis. Depending on the results of the analysis, some redesign or recoding may be required. Some additional documentation may be required, or some additional testing may be needed. In some cases, no changes at all may be the outcome where metrics only slightly exceed their target ranges and are deemed not critical.

It is important to understand what the metrics represent and not just accept them at face value. Understanding, insight, and confidence in the results can be achieved by delving into the conditions and circumstances that lead to the results reflected by metrics.

7.2.3.5   Validate the Software Quality Metrics

The purpose of validating the metrics is to gain confidence that the numbers reflect reality and to eventually begin to use certain metrics as predictors of those quality attributes (such as reliability) that cannot be measured during software development.

Validation of metric values is based on an assessment of the statistical significance of the metrics to the quality factors they represent. The details of this process are beyond the scope of this book. The reader is encouraged to refer to IEEE Standard 1061-1992 [2], which contains a thorough description of this process.

7.3   Metrics that support software verification activities

A number of metrics support the software V&V activities described in this book. A few examples are discussed here.

7.3.1   Complexity

Through experience, we have learned that the more complex code is, the more difficult it is to maintain, understand, document, test, and support [3–5]. Complexity is a direct metric that can be associated with the quality subfactor correctability and the quality factor maintainability, as shown in Table 7.10

Table 7.10   Complexity as a Direct Metric

Quality Factor	Quality Subfactor	Direct Metric
Maintainability: An attribute that bears on the effort needed for specific modifications.	Correctability: The degree of effort required to correct errors in software and cope with user complaints.	*Complexity*

Adapted from: [2]. © 1993 IEEE.

By application of a complexity measure to a wide sample of the code produced, an organization can establish a complexity baseline. This baseline represents the norm for the organization, which may be very different from the norms for other organizations. Once established, this norm can then be used to identify:

- Candidate modules for code inspections;
- Areas where redesign may be appropriate;
- Areas where additional documentation is required;
- Areas where additional testing may be required.

Complexity measures can also be used for a product baseline, which will be discussed in Chapter 8. In that way, one can see how the complexity of the entire product changes as the product evolves throughout the software development process.

Now that we have discussed ways in which complexity measures can be used, let's look at how complexity can be measured.

7.3.1.1 McCabe cyclomatic complexity metric

The McCabe cyclomatic complexity metric [6] uses the control flow structure of a program as a relative measure of its complexity. The cyclomatic complexity is computed as:

$$\text{cyclomatic complexity} = E - N + 2P$$

where

E = number of edges (or transfers of control)

P = number of control paths into the program

N = number of nodes (sequential groups of statements containing only one transfer of control)

To use this metric effectively, it is necessary to establish a complexity baseline by measuring cyclomatic complexity on as much of your organization's code as possible. Once you have established a baseline, look for modules whose cyclomatic complexity falls outside your baseline.

Several tools are commercially available tools that compute cyclomatic complexity. (See the section "Further Information," at the end of this chapter.)

7.3.1.2 Halstead's software science

Rather than use a program's structure to compute complexity, Halstead [7] developed an algorithm for measuring complexity based on a program's size expressed in terms of the number of unique operators and operands used.

Given the following parameters about a program:

η_1 = number of distinct operators

η_2 = number of distinct operands

N_1 = number of occurrences of operators

N_2 = number of occurrences of operands

The results produced include:

η = program vocabulary = $\eta_1 + \eta_2$

Several tools are commercially available that compute Halstead's software science complexity metric.

7.3.2 Defect metrics

Defect metrics are collected from Inspection Summary reports. Categorizing these metrics by defect type (logic, interface, data definition, documentation, etc.), origin, and severity will identify areas of the software development process that need improvement.

Another way defect metrics support software V&V activities is by tracking defects by module. This method can identify modules that may be candidates for redesign or require additional testing. This method potentially can also identify software engineers who may need additional training in good software engineering practices.

7.3.3   Product metrics

Product metrics are measures that represent the product your organization has developed. These measurements are essential for software V&V activities and adjusting some of those activities accordingly.

Examples of some key product metrics to collect during the development phase include:

- Number and type of defects found during requirements, design, code, and test inspections;
- Number of pages of documentation delivered;
- Number of new source lines of code created;
- Number of source lines modified;
- Total number of source lines of code delivered;
- Average complexity of all modules delivered;
- Average size of modules;
- Total number of modules;
- Total number of bugs found as a result of unit testing;
- Total number of bugs found as a result of integration testing;
- Total number of bugs found as a result of validation testing;
- Productivity, as measured by KLOC per person-hour.

For example, you may want to adjust the nature and the type of regression testing performed based on the number of source lines modified. You may need to add additional tests based on the average complexity of the code.

Tying these measures to product baselines (which are discussed in Chapter 8) can provide insights into the nature of your product and your software development process. This information can be used to help drive further process improvements.

7.3.4   Process metrics

Process metrics are intended to reflect the effectiveness of your processes. By collecting these measures and analyzing the results over several projects, you can identify trends, which should lead to process improvements.

Examples of some key process metrics to collect include:

- Defect correction time;
- Number of person-hours per inspection;
- Number of person-hours per KLOC;
- Average number of defects found per inspection;
- Number of defects found during inspections in each defect category;
- Average amount of rework time;
- Percentage of modules that were inspected.

For example, by analyzing the defects found during code inspections, you may find that the same type of defect occurs frequently. To remedy that problem, you can develop a new coding standard that would help prevent this defect from occurring on future projects. The defect correction time can be used as leverage to institute more effective defect detection and prevention techniques on future projects.

7.4 Summary

When instituting a measurement program, and organization should consider the following set of attributes, suggested by Humphrey [8]:

- The measures should be robust.
- The measures should suggest a norm.
- The measures should relate to specific product and process properties.
- The measures should suggest an improvement strategy.
- The measures should be a natural result of the software development process.
- The measures should be simple.
- The measures should be predictable and trackable.
- The measures should not be used as part of an employee's performance evaluation.

Measurements support basic software quality improvement principles. Measurements can provide the leverage to drive software process improvements. However, unless a company establishes aggressive quality improvement plans and goals, nothing will change. Most important, those goals must be quantitative.

It is important to recognize the difference between *change* and *improvement*. Improvement is based on measurement, while change is based on perception. The way to know that a change is an improvement is through measurement.

REFERENCES

[1] Grady, R. B., and D. L. Caswell, *Software Metrics: Establishing a Company-Wide Program*, Englewood-Cliffs, NJ: Prentice-Hall, 1987.

[2] IEEE Standard 1061-1992, *IEEE Standard for a Software Quality Metrics Methodology*, 1993.

[3] McCabe, T. J., and C. W. Butler, "Design Complexity Measurement and Testing," *Communications of the ACM*, Vol. 32, No. 12, 1989, pp. 1415–1425.

[4] Walsh, T. I., "Software Readability Study Using a Complexity Measure," *Proceedings of the National Computer Conference*, New York: AFIPS, 1979.

[5] Ward, W. T., "Software Defect Prevention Using McCabe's Cyclomatic Complexity Metric," *Hewlett-Packard Journal*, April 1989, pp. 64–69.

[6] McCabe, T. J., "Complexity Measure," *IEEE Trans. Software Engineering*, Vol. SE-2, No. 4, 1976, pp. 308–320.

[7] Halstead, H. M., *Elements of Software Science*, New York: North-Holland, 1977.

[8] Humphrey, W. S., *Managing the Software Process*, Reading, MA: Addison-Wesley, 1989, p. 308.

Further information

At the time of publication, information on commercially available tools for measuring complexity could be found on the World Wide Web at the following addresses.

- *The home page for McCabe and Associates:* http://www.mccbe.com ;
- *The home page for Setlabs, Inc.:* http://www.molalla.net/~setlabs .

See also Brian Marick's list published periodically in the Usenet discussion group: comp.software.testing.

Chapter 8

Configuration management

The most frustrating software problems are often caused by poor configuration management. The problems are frustrating because that take time to fix, they often happen at the worst time, and they are totally unnecessary.

W. S. Humphrey,
Managing the Software Process,
Reading, MA: Addison-Wesley, 1989

THE VERAZANNO NARROWS BRIDGE, which connects Staten Island to Brooklyn, is the longest suspension bridge in the world, with a center span of 4,260 feet. The $325 million project was started in 1959 and was scheduled to be completed in 1965. The project was actually completed in November 1964, under budget and ahead of schedule.

Why is it that over 30 years ago we were able to complete such an incredible engineering feat on time and under budget, but today we have difficulty delivering software to customers on time and with features customers want?

What can we learn from building bridges that can be applied to building software? We know that:

- Software is conceptual and intangible, whereas bridges are physical and very tangible.

- To build a bridge, you need a well-defined and documented process.

- The process identifies all the parts needed, usually in the form of a bill of materials, and includes a detailed assembly procedure. The assembly procedure usually includes an exploded parts diagram, which shows how all the parts fit together.

Many people have a hard time understanding why software is so difficult to build. This lack of understanding often leads to:

- Lack of control;

- Lack of monitoring;

- Lack of traceability;

- Uncontrolled changes.

When more than two people work on the same software project, there is a real potential that their work will conflict. These conflicts can be in one or more of the following areas [1]:

- *Simultaneous update:* How can you prevent one person from inadvertently undoing the changes of another?

- *Shared and common code:* How do you ensure that all users are notified when a bug is fixed in code shared by several people? How do you notify everyone that bugs found in common code have been fixed?

- *Versions:* On large projects, several versions of the product may exist at the same time. When a bug is found and fixed in one version, how to you determine if the same bug exists in other versions? How do you ensure that the fix is made to all affected versions?

To prevent these conflicts, some form of process control is required. This chapter discusses the activities that make up *software configuration management* (SCM). SCM is a key software verification activity.

8.1 Software configuration management basics

SCM is a set of management disciplines performed within the context of the software development process. Critical SCM functions fall into three categories: identification, baseline management, and auditing and reporting.

- The identification functions address a wide range of issues related to identifying the software configuration items included in a baseline as well as identifying baselines themselves. These functions are discussed in Section 8.2.

- As software configuration items are built to form baselines, those baselines must be managed and controlled. Criteria for defining, building, and managing baselines are all part of the baseline management function. Baseline management is addressed in Section 8.3.

- The auditing and reporting functions address issues related to ensuring that what we think is included in a baseline actually is as well as providing a level of assurance that SCM procedures are being followed throughout the project. These functions are discussed in Section 8.4.

SCM provides a common point of integration for all planning, oversight, and implementation activities for a product, which usually includes software, user documentation (both printed and on-line), and various forms of media, including CD-ROM, floppy disk, tape, *electrically programmable read only memory* (EPROM), and printed materials.

There are several excellent references on SCM [1–4], and two ANSI/IEEE Standards address the subject. ANSI/IEEE Standard 828-1983 [5] outlines an SCM plan, and ANSI/IEEE Standard 1042-1987 [6] includes a thorough overview of SCM as well as examples of SCM plans that would be appropriate for an embedded software application, a small experimental software project, and a software maintenance activity.

As with any other activity that is worth doing, SCM activities must be planned. The two ANSI/IEEE Standards mentioned here are excellent resources for developing an SCM plan for a given project.

8.1.1 Definitions

Some key SCM terms defined in ANSI/IEEE Standard 1042-1987 [6] are:

- *Baseline.* A baseline is a milestone in the software development process marked by the delivery of one or more software configuration items. A baseline consists of software configuration item(s) that have been formally reviewed and agreed on and that thereafter serves as the basis for further development. A baseline can be changed only through formal change control procedures.

- *Software configuration item.* A software configuration item is a collection of software elements treated as a unit for the purposes of configuration management.

- *Configuration.* A configuration is defined as consisting of a parts list and an exploded parts diagram that define all the elements of a baseline and how they fit together.

- *Configuration control board (CCB).* The CCB is responsible for reviewing and approving changes to baselines. The CCB usually consists of representatives of the project team.

- *Software.* Software, in the context of configuration management, is defined as information structured with logical and functional properties. It is created and maintained in many forms and representations over the course of its development.

- *Version.* A version is a specific instance of a baseline or a software configuration item.

8.1.2 An example of a manufacturing process

To manufacture a product, you need a manufacturing process, which includes three things: a *bill of material* (BOM), a detailed assembly procedure, and an exploded parts diagram.

Examples of a real BOM and an exploded parts diagram for something we are familiar with (a lawnmower) are shown in Figures 8.1 and 8.2.

Look closely at the information that is included in the figures. The BOM in Figure 8.1 identifies each part with a part number. The exploded parts diagram in Figure 8.2 graphically illustrates how all the parts fit together. With this information and a detailed assembly procedure, you have enough information to assemble the parts and build a lawnmower.

If we apply a manufacturing process to building software, we will need a parts list that represents all of the "software parts" needed to "build" the product. We will need an exploded parts diagram that shows where the parts are and how they fit together. Figures 8.3 and 8.4 are examples of a software parts list and an exploded parts diagram. In addition, we need to create a build procedure that can be used to make the product. A build procedure may be as

REF. NO.	PART NO.	CODE	DESCRIPTION	REF. NO.	PART NO.	CODE	DESCRIPTION
1	747-0824		Control Handle Ass'y. (Std.)	34	736-0452		Bell-Wash. .39" I.D.
	647-0004		Control Handle Ass'y. (Deluxe)	35	710-1055		Hex Bolt 3/8-24 x 1" Lg.
2	710-1205		Rope Guide	36	742-0621		21" Blade
3	720-0279		Handle Knob 1/4-20 Thd.		742-0721		21" Mulching Blade (Optional)
4	710-1174		Curved Hd. Bolt 5/16-18 x 2" Lg.	37	736-0169		L-Wash. 3/8" I.D.*
6	720-0276		Hand Knob	38	712-0241		Hex Nut 3/8-24 Thd.
7	710-0605		Oval C-Sunk Mach. Scr.	39	736-0356		Bell-Wash. .39" I.D. x 1.38"
8	736-0501		Spr. Wash. .66" I.D.	40	712-0798		Hex Nut 3/8-16 Thd.*
9	712-0324		Hex L-Nut 1/4-20 Thd.	41	15261A		Height Adj. Plate
10	746-0876		Throttle Lever	42	15262B		Pivot Bar
11	749-0538C		Upper Handle	43	14832		Spring Lever Ass'y. w/Knob
12	720-0226		Foam Grip (Optional)	44	738-0507B		Shld. Bolt .5" Dia. x .357"
13	749-0928		Lower Handle	45	736-0105		Bell-Wash. .38" I.D. x .88" O.D.
14	726-0240		Cable Tie	46	738-0102		Axle Bolt
15	764-0310		Rear Catcher Frame†	47	720-0190		Spring Lever Knob
16	746-0550		Control Cable—39" (410, 412, 414, 424)	48	732-0417A		Spring Lever
	746-0737		Control Cable—51" (411, 413, 423, 425)	49	14578		Height Adj. Ass'y. Comp.—R.H.
	746-0553		Control Cable—36" (416, 418, 426, 428)		14579		Height Adj. Ass'y. Comp.—L.H. (Not Shown)
17	746-0842		Throttle Control Wire—51" (410, 412, 414, 424)	50	14765		Pivot Bar
	746-0847		Throttle Control Wire—42" (411, 413, 423, 425)	51	782-5002		Front Baffle
	746-0843		Throttle Control Wire—55" (416, 418, 426, 428)	52	710-0654		Hex L-Wash. Hd. Scr. 3/8-16 x 1" Lg.
18	764-0311		Front Catcher Frame†	53	782-5003		Rear Baffle
19	764-0309		Grass Bag†	54	710-1017		Torx Mach. AB-Tap Scr. 1/4 x .62" Lg.
	764-0457		Grass Bag w/Logo†	55	710-0892		Hex L-Wash. Hd. AB-Tap Scr. 1/4 x .62" Lg.
20	714-0104		Int. Cotter Pin 5/16" Dia.	56	682-0516		Handle Brkt. Ass'y.—R.H.
21	732-0678		Door Spring—R.H.	57	682-0515		Handle Brkt. Ass'y.—L.H.
22	732-0677		Door Spring—L.H.	58	782-0310		21" R.D. Deck
23	782-7000		Rear Discharge Door	59	**		Wheel Ass'y. Comp.
24	751B213146		Cable Clamp	60	**		Hub Cap
	7510007755		Casing Clamp (Tec.)	61	764-0433		Grass Bag††
25	646-0875		Throttle Body	62	731-1322		Hard Top Cover††
26	811-00185		Throttle Box Comp. (Incl. Ref. 7, 8, 9, 10, 25)	63	710-0286		Pan Hd. Mach. Scr. 1/4-20 x .5" Lg.††
27	—		Engine	64	712-0324		Hex Nylon L-Nut 1/4-20 Thd.††
28	710-1237		Hex Wash. Hd. Scr. #10-32 x .62" Lg.	65	782-9011		Mounting Bracket†
	710-0871		Hex Sems Scr. #10-32 x .3" Lg. (Tec.)	66	782-5007		Mulching Baffle Plug (Optional)
29	735-0639		Spark Plug Boot (Optional)	67	782-5004		Mulching Baffle—R.R. (Optional)
30	732-0700		Wire Rod	68	731-1405		Deflector (Optional)
31	731-1236		Rear Flap	69	711-0996		Rod (Optional)
32	753-0484		Blade Adapter Kit	70	726-0201		Push Speed Nut (Optional)
33	710-1044		Hex Bolt 3/8-24 x 1.5" Lg.	71	710-0192		Truss Scr. #10-24 x .38" Lg.
				72	720-0275		Knob
				73	731-1506		Deck Shroud (Optional)†
				76	748-0376		Blade Adapter (416 Only)
				77	736-0524		Blade Bell Support (416 Only)

Figure 8.1 Parts list for a lawnmower.

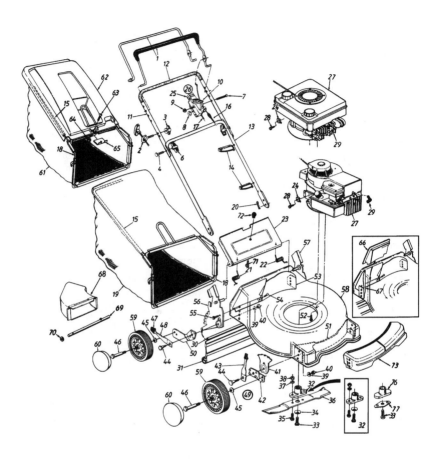

Figure 8.2   Exploded parts diagram for a lawnmower.

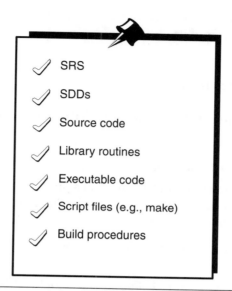

Figure 8.3   A software parts list.

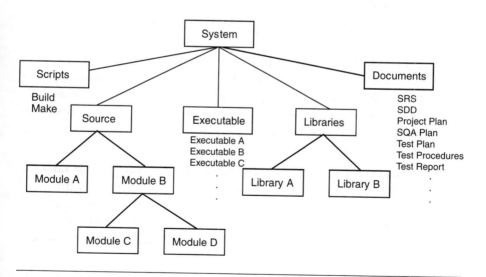

Figure 8.4   A software exploded parts diagram.

simple as a make script or as complicated as a document that describes the steps required to make the product.

8.2 Identification

Identification includes the functions associated with naming, labeling, and version control.

8.2.1 Naming and labeling

Identification determines how all the parts of a product are identified and how baselines built from the parts are identified. The following are key points regarding identification:

- Each software configuration item must be identified and uniquely labeled.
- The identification and labeling scheme should reflect the structure of the product.
- Criteria for identifying and labeling software configuration items need to be established.
- Criteria for identifying and labeling all forms of tests and test data need to be established.
- Criteria for identifying support tools used to build baselines need to be established. It is important to include the compilers, linkers, assemblers, make files, and other tools used to translate the software and build baselines. That ensures that you can always recreate the exact information produced by those tools long after they have been changed, replaced, or updated.
- Special attention may be needed for third-party or purchased software that is incorporated into your company's product, especially if any copyright or royalty issues are involved. Criteria should be established for how third-party or purchased software will be integrated into a product in a manner that will allow the software to be easily removed, replaced, or updated.
- Special attention may be needed for software that is being reused from other products or software that is intended to be reused.
- Special attention may be needed for prototype software that is intended to be replaced.

8.2.2 Version control

Version control provides support for parallel development by enabling branching and merging. Parallel development is important several reasons:

- It allows different projects to use the same source files at the same time.
- It isolates work that is not ready to be shared by the rest of the project.
- It isolates work that should never be shared (i.e., fixing a bug that exists only in an older release).
- It allows software engineers to continue development along a branch even when a line of development is frozen (e.g., during software validation testing).

To support parallel development, SCM tools need to support branching, file comparison, and merging functions.

Branching is an SCM function in which a configuration item (usually code) evolves simultaneously along two or more branches, with new versions added independently to each branch. This concept is illustrated in Figure 8.5.

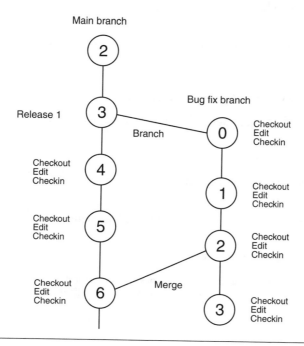

Figure 8.5   Branching and merging.

File comparison is a facility that compares files with the same name in two or more different branches or baselines and identifies those files that are different.

Merging is the process of selectively applying changes made to source files in branches or other baselines to the corresponding source files in the main branch.

Branching, file comparison, and merging are key functions for supporting SCM, especially for larger projects.

Supporting the version control functions is a version control procedure that provides a mechanism for making changes to a known baseline in a controlled manner. Key requirements of this procedure include:

- Proposed changes to baselines must have some level of review.
- The impacts (on cost, schedule, software development, manufacturing, etc.) of proposed changes must be identified and understood.
- Where appropriate, approval of the CCB, key managers, and/or project team members must be obtained.
- Approved changes must be properly implemented.

Once changes have been approved, all affected parties are notified of the changes.

8.2.3 Software configuration items

Examples of software configuration items are shown in Table 8.1.

Table 8.1 Examples of Software Configuration Items

Items	Related Information
Product concept specification	
Software project plans	Software development plan Software QA plan (SQAP) SCM plan Software V&V plan (SVVP)
SRS	
SDDs	

Items	Related Information
Source code	Source listings Executable files Make files Libraries
Database descriptions	Schema and file description Initial content
SCM procedures	Source tree structure Daily build procedures Backup procedures Software problem reports
Software release process	Internal release process External release process Release documentation
Software test documents	Test plans Test procedures Test scripts Test data Test reports
User documentation	User manuals On-line help System administration documentation Service documents
Maintenance documentation	Software maintenance plan Software problem reports Change requests

8.3 Baseline management

Baseline management applies to the many different types of baselines. It includes managing the workspace of individual developers, assessing changes to baselines, managing incomplete versions of software during development, and managing versions of the product once they are ready to be released to customers (also referred to as release engineering). Each type of baseline is discussed next.

Creating and managing baselines is an effective way to allow many people to work concurrently. Baseline management basics are discussed here in the form of FAQs.

8.3.1   Baseline management FAQs

What baselines are required to be defined and managed?

Baselines are typically are aligned with major milestones on projects. It is important to apply the baseline concept to documents as well as to code. For example, there may be a requirements baseline, which represents the approved SRS; a design baseline, which represents the approved SDD; and several code baselines. Each version of software produced by the software engineering group constitutes a baseline. During the software validation phase, the ability to control changes to code and, thus, manage baselines is extremely important, as we will see in Chapter 9.

How is the current software configuration defined?

The current software configuration can be thought of as a snapshot of everything the project has produced at some point in time. It can include documents, software (source, object, executables), tests, and user information. Specifically for software, a configuration is defined in terms of the functionality it embodies at the time the snapshot is taken. That functionality changes over time and should be measured against the requirements defined in the SRS.

Who must approve changes to baselines?

In many organizations, a CCB has responsibility and authority for approving changes to baselines. The CCB consists of people representing a cross-section of the project and typically includes software engineering, software QA, project management, technical publications, manufacturing, and other functions as appropriate. This board is empowered to review and approve changes to the various baselines defined in the project plan. The CCB also has responsibility for communicating approved changes to the rest of the organization, thus helping to make software development more visible and tangible.

How and where are baselines created and physically controlled?

Document baselines are created and controlled by the use of a document control system. Such a system consists of procedures that define how documents are reviewed, approved, and changed in a controlled manner. Software tools to control document baselines may be used if appropriate.

Code baselines are always created with a configuration control tool. Many tools are commercially available for creating and controlling changes to code.

In addition to tools, procedures are required to reinforce the tools. Once a baseline has been created, software engineers must be prevented from making unapproved changes.

How are people informed of changes?

Communicating changes often is a difficult problem. Not everyone is interested or needs to know details of every change made to the product. One of the functions of the CCB should be to disseminate approved changes to the project in an appropriate manner.

How are baselines verified?

Baselines are verified by examination (in the case of document baselines) or by inspection and testing (in the case of code base-lines). Because the features the baseline is supposed to implement are known, the task of verifying the baseline against known features is conceptually straightforward.

Are baselines tied to project milestones?

Many baselines are tied to project milestones. Document baselines usually are tied to project milestones such as "requirements defined" or "design completed." But there are also many baselines that may not be tied to a specific milestone. During the coding phase, many baselines may be created. A few may be tied to a specific milestone, such as code freeze, but most are not. As we will see in Chapter 9, during software validation testing , several baselines can be created as bugs are fixed and verified.

Baselines that are tied to project milestones should be identified in the project plan.

What information is required to process a change to a baseline?

The information required to approve a change to a baseline should be defined by the CCB. For a document baseline, typically the information required might include a list of all the pages that have changed, a summary of the changes, and the change pages, showing the actual changes to the text.

During the course of a software development project, many baselines are created. One of the most important tasks associated with creating new baselines is an assessment of the differences between them. Knowing what has changed from one baseline is essential. If problems are encountered in a new baseline, the first question that is asked is what has changed from the previous baseline.

For software baselines, there are two reasons to make changes to code: adding functionality and fixing bugs. When functionality is added, identification of the specific features being added is important when a change to the baseline is being processed. When bugs are fixed, the specific bugs fixed and the modules affected by the fix should be provided when a change to the baseline is processed.

This becomes especially crucial during the software validation testing phase of the project, when there needs to be tight control over changes to software. Many projects have a code freeze milestone. After code freeze, the only changes that should be made to the software are changes in response to bugs reported from testing activities. With this level of control, you can associate code changes to bug fixes for purposes of conducting so-called mini-inspections to ensure that bug fixes have not inadvertently introduced new bugs. You can also identify changes to source code by module from one baseline to the next. By doing this and by then comparing the list of changed modules to the bug reports that were supposed to have been fixed, you can determine if any unapproved changes were made to the code.

What tools, resources, and training are required to perform baseline change assessments?

Tools required to perform a baseline change assessment for code baselines are relatively simple. As mentioned earlier, a file comparison tool that can identify changes to source across baselines and provide a list of changed modules is required. Many commercially available tools can provide this information. Resources and training required to do this assessment will of course vary, based on project size and complexity. The group that is managing baselines should be the group that provides the baseline change assessment information. It makes sense for the software QA group to perform the analysis of this information and report the results to the project team or the CCB.

What metrics should be used to assess changes to a baseline?

In trying to determine if changes to a software baseline should be accepted, it is helpful to apply a basic set of metrics to the baseline to provide the CCB or project management team with additional information. Examples of these kinds of metrics are:

- Complexity;
- Average module size;
- Number of modules changed;

- Number of bugs fixed and verified;
- Code coverage.

Additional information on these metrics is included in Chapter 10.

How are unauthorized changes to source code prevented, detected, and corrected?

It is not possible to prevent unauthorized changes to source code. Software engineers love nothing more than a technical challenge. Advertising that your system can prevent unwanted changes presents such a challenge. A far better approach is to provide software engineers with training and an understanding of why unapproved changes are not good for the project. Using a commercially available SCM tool will provide an adequate degree of security.

The baseline change assessment procedure described in Section 8.3.3 can be used to detect unauthorized changes to code baselines. These changes should be presented to the project team and the CCB for resolution.

What tools, resources, and training are required to perform baseline management?

A fully featured SCM tool is an absolute requirement for almost every software development project. Several SCM tools are commercially available that can provide the level of control required for many types of project.

The scope and the size of a project will determine the resources required for SCM functions. In some organizations, SCM responsibilities are performed by the software engineering group. This approach may work well for small projects, but it quickly falls apart on larger projects where communication and timeliness of information are key. SCM functions can be effectively performed as part of a software QA group. On larger projects, there may be justification for a separate SCM group.

Everyone involved with producing documents and software will require some SCM training, which can range from basic SCM principles to the details of using SCM tools.

8.3.2 Workspace management

Software engineers need to have a consistent and reproducible workspace area they can use for development activity. This workspace area (commonly called a *play area* or a *sandbox*) allows developers to develop and debug their code while sharing those files that need to be shared and shielding the rest of the project from the inherent instability of evolving code. SCM tools used on most projects need to support this capability.

8.3.3 Baseline change assessment

Another baseline management function that should be supported by the SCM tools is baseline change assessment. This assessment provides an effective way to manage changes to software and can be used throughout the development phase, especially during the software validation testing phase.

During development, new modules that are integrated into a baseline will frequently have undesirable effects. A baseline change assessment helps identify those modules most recently integrated, to determine where the problems are.

During software validation testing , the baseline change assessment is used to ensure that the only changes made to the code are changes associated with bug fixes. By comparing the source files of the current version with the previous version, you can identify the modules that have changed. If you then match the changed modules with the affected modules indicated on your bug reports, you can determine if only those modules that should have changed did change.

8.3.4 Version management

An essential SCM function is reliably building and re-creating versions of the product as it evolves and after it is released. During development, incomplete versions of the product are built and tested on a regular basis. The SCM tools need to be able to re-create previous versions exactly, because frequently it may be desirable to retreat to a previous version. Once development is complete, the SCM tools need to manage the versions of software that are released to customers. All necessary information (including the specific compilers, linkers, and other tools used) must be maintained, to ensure that each released version of the product can be recreated.

8.4 Auditing and reporting

Auditing and reporting procedures are intended to provide assurance that the software product matches the software configuration items (software and documents). These procedures typically can include such activities as ensuring that the source code and the software documentation match and that the software and the user documentation match.

Auditing and reporting procedures help answer the questions shown in Table 8.2.

Table 8.2 Questions Answered by Auditing and Reporting

Are there mechanisms to provide an audit trail such as change histories?

Does more than one type of audit need to be performed for each baseline?

How are subcontractors involved in an audit?

How are third-party software configuration items managed, controlled, and audited?

Is there a separate audit trail for each baseline? For each component? For each functional group?

What are the audit trail requirements imposed by other organizations such as customers, regulatory agencies, and corporate policies?

What tools, resources, and training are required to perform each type of audit?

What type of information needs to be maintained after product development is complete and for how long?

How is software (in its physical media form) retained?

Are secure storage facilities required?

Is media protected from disaster? How?

Auditing and reporting tasks include those associated with auditing, reporting, and records collection and retention.

8.4.1 Auditing

Audits are one way an organization can ensure that the project team has done all the required work in a way that satisfies customer requirements and external obligations. During the course of a software development project, several different types of audits may be performed, including in-process audits, *functional audits* (FAs), physical audits (PAs), and quality systems audits. Several attributes of each type of audits are listed in Table 8.3.

8.4.2 Configuration status accounting

A configuration status accounting procedure consists of mechanisms for capturing status information regarding each configuration item and for reporting that status information in a timely manner. Configuration status accounting becomes a critical task as the size and the complexity of projects increase. The reports that are produced are most frequently used by project management to assess the current status of a project.

Key requirements of this procedure include:

- Identifying the types of information that project managers need;
- Identifying the degree of control needed by project management;
- Identifying the reports required and the different audiences for each report;
- Identifying the information required to produce each report.

Table 8.3   Types of Audits

Attribute	In-Process Audit	Functional Audit	Physical Audit	Quality Systems Audit
Objective	To verify the consistency of the design as it evolves through the development process	To verify that functionality and performance are consistent with requirements defined in the SRS	To verify that the as-built version of software and documentation are internally consistent and ready for delivery	To independently assess compliance to the SQAP
Materials required	SRS; SDDs; source code; waivers; approved changes; software V&V plan (SVVP); test results	SRS; executable code; waivers; test programs; software V&V reports; in-process audit reports; test documentation; completed tests; planned tests	Waivers; architecture; SRS and SDDs; approved changes; acceptance test documentation; customer documentation; approved product labeling; software version; FA reports	SQAP; all documents associated with software development activities

Attribute	In-Process Audit	Functional Audit	Physical Audit	Quality Systems Audit
Activities	Hardware and software interfaces consistent with SRS and SDDs; code fully tested to SVVP; evolving design matches SRS; code consistent with SDDs	Audit test documentation against test data; audit software V&V report; ensure results of reviews have been incorporated.	Audit SRS; FA reports for actions taken; sample SDDs for completeness; audit customer manuals for completeness and consistency; software delivery media and controls	Examine quality program documents; selective compliance testing; interview staff; perform in-process audits; examine FA and PA reports
Results	In-process audit reports noting all discrepancies	FA report recommending approval, contingent approval or disapproval	PA report recommending approval, contingent approval, or disapproval	Overall evaluation of compliance with the software quality program

8.4.3 Reports, records collection, and retention

As each audit is performed, the results are reported and distributed to the project team. Records collection procedures identify the specific information that needs to be collected, and retention procedures define how long the information should be kept.

8.5 Summary

No matter where you are in the system lifecycle, the system will change and the desire to change it will persist throughout the life cycle.

E. H. Bersoff et al.,
Software Configuration Management,
Englewood Cliffs, NJ: Prentice-Hall, 1980

Some key points regarding SCM are:

- Change is inevitable.
- Defined procedures are required to manage change effectively without preventing change from occurring.
- Software, because it exists in many different forms, presents many challenges from a control, management, and tracking perspective.
- It is important to know what you have and how you got there.
- It is essential to be able to re-create exactly what is delivered to customers.

Maintaining project deliverables throughout the product life cycle (which can be many years) is a key benefit of SCM. This benefit means that when (not if) you decide to make changes to your product, you will have the benefit of all available knowledge of the requirements, design, implementation, and test.

REFERENCES

[1]   Babich, W. A., *Software Configuration Management: Coordination for Team Productivity*, Reading, MA: Addison-Wesley, 1986.

[2]   Humphrey, W. S., *Managing the Software Process*, Reading, MA: Addison-Wesley, 1989.

[3]   Bryan, W., et al., *Software Configuration Management*, New York: IEEE Computer Society Press, 1980.

[4]   Bersoff, E. H., et. al., *Software Configuration Management*, Englewood-Cliffs, NJ: Prentice-Hall, 1980.

[5]   ANSI/IEEE Standard 828-1983, *IEEE Standard for Software Configuration Management Plans*, 1983, IEEE, Inc., 345 East 47th Street, NY, NY 10017.

[6]   ANSI/IEEE Standard 1042-1987, *IEEE Guide to Software Configuration Management*, 1988, IEEE, Inc., 345 East 47th Street, NY, NY 10017.

Part III: Overview of software validation activities

R<small>ECALL THE</small> definitions of verification and validation:

- *Verification* is "the process of determining whether or not the products of a given phase of the software development cycle fulfill the requirements established during the previous phase" [1], or in other words, "Are we building the product *right*?"

- *Validation* is "the process of evaluating software at the end of the software development process to ensure compliance with software requirements" [1], or in other words, "Did we build the *right* product?"

Validation activities are defined around three basic processes: testing, measurement, and software reliability growth. Chapter 9 discusses testing as a validation activity. Different levels of testing and the objectives of each level are discussed. As with any activity, the testing process needs to be planned. An outline for a software validation test plan is discussed, and references to several ANSI/IEEE Standards are provided.

Chapter 10 examines several measures that can help in the planning, scheduling, and management of the testing process.

Chapter 11 discusses the concept of software reliability growth in the context of providing information that can be used by management to help make decisions regarding when to stop testing and release the product.

REFERENCE

[1]   ANSI/IEEE Standard 729-1983, *IEEE Standard Glossary for Software Engineering Terminology*, 1983, IEEE, Inc., 345 East 47th Street, NY, NY 10017.

Chapter 9

Testing

Testing is the process of executing programs with the intention of finding errors.

G. J. Myers,
The Art of Software Testing,
New York: Wiley, 1976

Testing can show the presence of bugs but never their absence.

E. W. Dijkstra,
"Structured Programming,"
in *Software Engineering Techniques,*
edited by J. N. Buxton and B. Randell,
Brussels: NATO Science Committee, 1990

THESE OBSERVATIONS by Myers and Dijkstra illustrate common misconceptions about testing. Unfortunately, many people still think that testing can be used to demonstrate that their software does not have any bugs.

Myers offers the following example to illustrate how difficult it is to test software:

A program accepts as input three integer values. The three values represent the three sides of a triangle. Based on the three values, the program is to determine whether the triangle is isosceles, scalene, or equilateral. [1]

As an exercise, try writing down the set of test cases that you think would adequately test this simple program.

Myers identifies a set of test cases that would adequately test this program, most of which were based on actual errors detected in various versions of programs written for this exercise. After you have written down the tests you think are needed, refer to Appendix I, where the test cases are repeated. Compare your set with that in the appendix. On average, even experienced programmers think of only slightly more than half of the test cases needed. The point of the exercise is to illustrate just how difficult it is to develop a thorough set of test cases for a trivial program.

Consider another trivial program from Humphrey [2] that analyzes strings of alphabetic characters, 10 at a time. There are 26^{10} possible combinations of inputs this program could expect to see. Would it be feasible to test all the possible combinations of inputs? Let us take a look at exhaustive testing.

For this program, 26^{10} tests would be required. Assume it takes very little time to write these tests. If it took, on average, 1 microsecond to execute each test case, it would take about *4.5 million years* to execute all the tests. And this approach would not address many invalid cases, such as longer strings of characters.

Clearly, for most software products, where the size of the input space is many orders of magnitude larger than this trivial example, the time required to develop and execute such large numbers of tests cannot be economically justified, even if it were feasible.

So if we cannot do exhaustive testing, our objective then becomes to select a relatively small number of tests that have a high probability of finding defects. The obvious question is: how do you write tests that can do this?

There is no magic formula for writing tests that have a high probability of finding defects. There are, however, some good testing practices that should be followed to help maximize the benefit gained from the testing activity. These practices are summarized in Table 9.1.

Table 9.1 Good Testing Practices [1]

A good test case is one that has a high probability of detecting an undiscovered defect, not one that shows that the program works correctly.

It is impossible to test your own programs.

A necessary part of every test case is a description of the expected result.

Avoid nonreproducible or on-the-fly testing.

Write test cases for valid as well as invalid input conditions.

Thoroughly inspect the results of each test.

As the number of detected defects in a piece of software increases, the probability of the existence of more undetected defects also increases.

Assign the best people to do testing.

Ensure that testability is a key objective in the software design.

Never alter the program to make testing easier.

Testing, like almost every other activity, must start with objectives.

This chapter reviews the various levels of testing, the objectives of each, and the different test methods that are appropriate for each level of testing.

But first, for the testing activity to be productive, it must be carefully planned. To guide you in this task, an outline for a software validation test plan is included in Appendix H. Also included in Appendix H are examples of a software validation test procedure and a test report. The test plan in Appendix H is based on the ANSI/IEEE Standard 1012-1986, *Standard for Software Verification and Validation Plans* [3], and the recently released ANSI/IEEE 1059-1994 *Guide for Software Verification and Validation Plans* [4].

In addition, the first international Software Engineering Process Life Cycle standard is under development by the ISO as ISO-12207 [5]. This standard defines the necessary processes, activities, and tasks required to produce large, complex software systems. The standard defines three categories, which are further defined into 17 processes, 74 activities, and 224 tasks. This standard is anticipated to be one of the building blocks for international software trade. Deployment of the standard is well underway in the international software community.

9.1 Testing: levels and methods

9.1.1 Levels of testing

The various levels of testing form a hierarchy, as illustrated in Figure 9.1.

At the bottom of the hierarchy is unit, or module, testing. The overall objective of this level of testing is to find bugs in logic, data, and algorithms in individual modules.

After unit testing, the next level is usually called integration testing. Integration testing is intended to find bugs in interfaces between modules.

Moving up the hierarchy, the next level after integration testing is frequently called validation testing. Recall the definition of validation: "the process of evaluating software at the end of the software development process to ensure compliance with software requirements" [1]. The objective of validation testing is to determine if the software meets all its requirements (as defined in a document like an SRS).

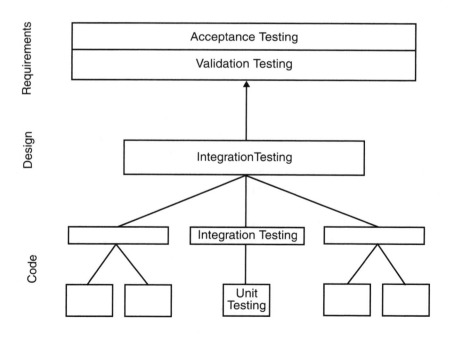

Figure 9.1   Testing hierarchy.

As part of validation testing, regression testing is performed to determine if the software still meets all its requirements in light of changes and modifications to the software. (Regression testing frequently is also performed during software development as new versions of the product are being developed.)

Finally, there may be another level of testing, referred to as acceptance testing. The objective of this level is to determine if the software meets customer requirements. Alpha and beta testing are variants of acceptance testing.

This chapter focuses on unit testing, integration testing and validation testing.

9.1.2 Test methods

Similar to the levels of testing, there are also several different testing methods. For example:

- *White box* or *glass box* testing is a method of testing in which knowledge of the software's internal design is used to develop tests.

- In *functional* or *black box* testing, no knowledge of software design is used, and tests are based strictly on requirements and functionality.

- *Top-down, bottom-up,* and *outside-in* testing are all examples of different methods for performing incremental integration testing whereby modules are integrated and tested based on their positions in the module hierarchy.

- *Act-like-a-customer* (ALAC) testing is a method in which tests are developed based on knowledge of how customers use the software product. ALAC tests are based on the principle that complex software products have many bugs. To maximize benefit to customers, defect detection and correction activities should focus on those bugs customers are likely to find (Figure 9.2).

Table 9.2 summarizes levels of testing and test methods that are most appropriate for each level.

9.2 Testing procedures

This section looks at some specific procedures that can be used for the various testing levels.

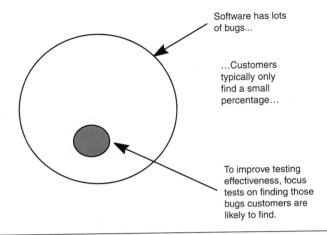

Figure 9.2   Act like a customer testing.

Table 9.2   Testing Levels and Test Methods

Level	Objective	Performed by	Test Environment	Test Methods
Unit	Find bugs in logic, data and algorithms in individual modules	Software engineers	Isolated; stubs and scaffolding may be required	White box
Integration	Find bugs in interfaces between modules	Software engineers	Isolated and/or simulated; stubs and scaffolding required.	White box top-down, bottom-up, or outside-in
Validation	Determine if software meets SRS	Software QA; software validation team	Actual (may not have final hardware)	Functional and ALAC
Regression	Determine if software still meets SRS in light of changes	Software QA; software validation team	Actual (may not have final hardware)	Functional and ALAC
Acceptance	Determine if software meets customer requirements	Customer, software QA, and/or project team	Actual (usually at customer site)	Functional and ALAC (customer may have own tests)

9.2.1 Unit Testing

The objective of unit testing is to find bugs in individual modules. Unit testing is usually considered part of the coding process and usually requires a significant investment in *scaffolding*, as illustrated in Figure 9.3. Unfortunately, unit testing is often viewed more as a debugging activity rather than a testing activity.

The difference between debugging and testing is important. Debugging is defined as "the process of locating, analyzing, and correcting suspected faults" [6]. Testing, on the other hand, is defined as "the process of exercising or evaluating a system or a system component by manual or automated means to verify that it satisfies specified requirements or to identify differences between expected and actual results" [6].

In many organizations, unit testing is an informal activity performed by software engineers on their own modules with little or no test documentation. From a test methods standpoint, unit testing clearly requires a white box approach.

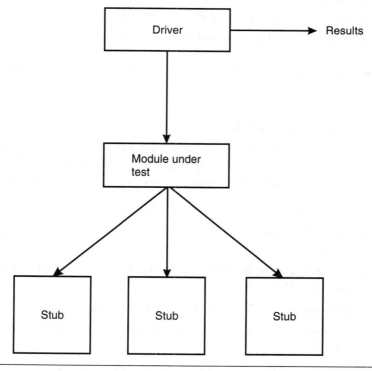

Figure 9.3 Unit testing environment.

To help improve the effectiveness of unit testing, the following questions can act as a checklist during the examination of unit tests written by software engineers:

- *Algorithms and logic:* Have algorithms and logic been correctly implemented?
- *Data structures (global and local):* Are global data structures used? If so, what assumptions are made regarding global data? Are these assumptions valid? Are local data used? Is the integrity of local data maintained during all steps of an algorithms execution?
- *Interfaces:* Do data from calling modules match what this module expects to receive? Do data from called modules match what this module provides?
- *Independent paths:* Are all independent paths through the module identified and exercised?
- *Boundary conditions:* Are the boundary conditions known and tested to ensure that the module operates properly at its boundaries?
- *Error handling:* Are all error-handling paths exercised?

IEEE Standard 1008-1987 [7] provides additional information on unit testing.

9.2.2 Integration testing

The objective of integration testing is to find bugs related to interfaces between modules as they are integrated. One question is frequently asked: If all modules are unit tested, why is integration testing necessary? Here are some answers:

- One module can adversely affect another module.
- Subfunctions, when combined, may not produce the desired major function.
- Individually acceptable imprecision in calculations may be magnified to unacceptable levels.
- Interfacing errors not detected in unit testing may appear.
- Timing problems (in real-time systems) are not detectable by unit testing.
- Unit testing cannot detect resource contention problems.

Integration testing covers a broad range of testing, beginning with the testing of a few modules and culminating with the testing of the complete system. Let us look briefly at different approaches to integration testing.

Incremental integration is a systematic approach to integration whereby the program is constructed and tested in small chunks so that errors are easy to observe, isolate, and correct. Incremental integration can be performed top-down, bottom-up, or outside-in.

In top-down integration, modules integrated by moving downward through the program hierarchy, starting with the topmost or main module. Modules are integrated as illustrated in Figure 9.4. Top-down integration, as defined by Pressman [8], is performed as follows:

1. Use the main control module as a driver, and substitute stubs for all modules directly subordinate to the main module.
2. Depending on the integration approach selected (depth first or breadth first), replace subordinate stubs with modules one at a time.
3. Run tests as each individual module is integrated.
4. On the successful completion of a set of tests, replace another stub with a real module.
5. Perform regression testing to ensure that errors have not developed as a result of integrating new modules.
6. Repeat the process from step 2 until the whole program is integrated.

There are some inherent problems with top-down integration, as described by Pressman [8]:

- Many times, calculations are performed in the modules at the bottom of the hierarchy.
- Stubs typically do not pass data up to the higher modules.
- Delaying testing until lower level modules are ready usually results in integrating many modules at the same time rather than one at a time.
- Developing stubs that can pass data up is almost as much work as developing the actual module.

This leads to another integration approach, called bottom-up integration. Pressman [8] defines the bottom-up integration procedure as follows:

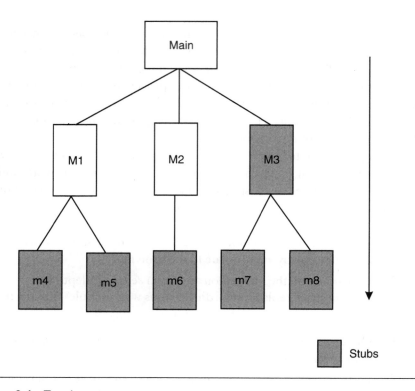

Figure 9.4   Top down integration testing environment.

1. Begin integration with the lowest level modules and combine them into clusters or builds that perform a specific software subfunction.
2. Write drivers (control programs developed as stubs) to coordinate test case input and output.
3. Test the cluster.
4. Remove the drivers and combine the clusters, moving upward in the program structure.

Just like the top-down approach, the bottom-up approach has drawbacks, some of which are:

- The whole program does not exist until the last module is integrated.
- Timing and resource contention problems are not found until late in the process.

The outside-in approach attempts to combine the advantages of top-down and bottom-up integration. In this approach, critical modules are integrated in a top-down manner, while noncritical modules are integrated from the bottom up. The drawbacks to the outside-in approach are:

- Both stubs and drivers must be developed.
- It is difficult to decide which modules are critical and which are noncritical.

Refer to ANSI/IEEE Standard 829-1983 [9] for more information on documenting the testing process.

9.2.3 Validation testing

The objective of software validation testing is to determine if the software meets its requirements as defined in the SRS and other relevant documents. Achieving that objective is based on the premise that software development and software validation tests are both based on the SRS.

The software validation testing process can be broken down into five phases:

1. Test planning;
2. Test development (informal validation);
3. Software validation readiness review;
4. Test execution (formal validation);
5. Test completion criteria.

Documenting the software validation testing process is important because much of the work that is performed to develop software validation tests will carry forward to future releases of the software. Three basic documents are associated with software validation:

- The software validation test plan defines the goals and objectives for the validation testing activity. The plan includes test estimates, resource requirements, and schedules.
- The software validation test procedure contains the detailed test scripts (automated and manual) that are to be executed.
- The software validation test report documents the results of formal validation testing.

Examples of all three documents are included in Appendix H.

Now let's look at each of the five phases of the software validation testing process.

9.2.3.1 Test planning

As with any other complex activity, software validation testing must begin with a plan. The plan drives the software validation activities from the beginning of test development through test completion (refer to Appendix H). Included in the test plan are the test estimates and schedules.

Test Estimates

Once the test plan has been written, the second phase can begin. It is during this phase that estimates of the numbers of tests required are made. These estimates are based on a review of the SRS and related documents. The number of tests required to adequately validate each requirement can be based on experience. This task can also be used to populate a *requirements traceability matrix* (RTM), which identifies each testable requirement and the test(s) associated with that requirement. Table 9.3 illustrates a portion of an RTM.

Table 9.3 Example of a Requirement Traceability Matrix

SRS paragraph	SDD paragraph	Test ID
4.1.1	4.2.4	4.1.1-01
4.1.2(a)	4.2.6	4.1.2-01
4.1.2(b)	4.2.7	4.1.2-02
etc.	...	...

As you review the SRS, estimate the number of tests required for each feature or function, taking into account such issues as the following:

- Test complexity;
- Different platforms;
- Automated or manual tests.

Use estimates from past projects to help develop new estimates. After each project, conduct a postmortem and look at the original estimates and the actual number of tests written. If there is a significant difference, investigate the reasons. Use the knowledge gained from this activity to improve your estimating skills for the next project.

Test Schedules

Once you have estimated the number of tests required, the next task is to estimate how much time and effort will be required to develop and execute these tests. Again, rely on past experience to develop accurate measures for the following:

- *Test development time:* the time required to develop and debug one test;
- *Test execution time:* the time required to execute one test.

Add an additional 25% to 50% of the time required to execute all the tests to allow for regression testing required due to big fixes during validation testing. The amount will vary, depending on factors such as how many inspections were held, integrity of the bug fixing process, amount of new code versus reused or modified code, amount of unit and integration testing performed, and so on.

Based on these three measures (number of tests required, test development time, and test execution time) and the available resources, you can develop a realistic software validation testing schedule. The schedule should be updated as project requirements change.

9.2.3.2   Test development (informal validation)

Test planning should be done early in the software development process, starting as early as the design phase. Once the planning is complete, test development can begin. Test development should occur in parallel with the coding phase of the project.

As coding and integration activities get underway, so can the informal validation testing. Informal validation testing is based on the ability of the software development group to provide incremental releases of the software to the validation testing group. Informal validation testing has the following objectives:

- It provides an opportunity for validation tests to be developed and debugged early in the software development process.
- It provides early feedback to software engineers.
- By the time coding is complete, all the validation tests should have been executed at least once, thereby increasing confidence that the software will meet all its requirements.

- It enables the formal validation testing activity to be less eventful, because most problems already will have been found.

Software validation test scripts define the detailed steps that demonstrate if the software meets a specific requirement. The test procedure is basically a collection of all the test scripts. An integral part of each test script is the expected results. An example of a test script is included in Appendix H.

In developing software validation tests, you should use several different test methods. Some examples follow.

- With white box testing, you use your knowledge of how the software is designed to maximize testing effectiveness by eliminating tests that test the same code (i.e., user interface).
- Use black box tests to test functionality and features.

The majority of your tests should be ALAC testing to help ensure that your testing uncovers those bugs customers are likely to find.

9.2.3.3 Software validation readiness review

Once the coding phases and informal validation have been completed, you should conduct a software validation readiness review. The purpose of this review is to ensure that everything is in place before the formal validation testing phase begins. This review helps ensure that validation testing begins only when the project is ready. Starting the formal validation testing prematurely will result in wasted effort, increased frustration, and pressure to release products.

SCM is essential for increasing the effectiveness of software validation testing. SCM tools provide a controlled environment and a mechanism for analyzing changes between baselines. Having the SCM tools in place and the code under version control are essential criteria for starting software validation testing.

The test plan should define the criteria that should be met *before* the formal validation testing can begin. Such criteria include the following.

- Software development has been completed.
- The software validation test plan has been reviewed and approved and is under document control.
- A requirements inspection has been performed on the SRS.
- Design inspections have been performed on the SDDs.
- Code inspections have been performed on all critical modules.

- All test scripts have been completed, and the software validation test procedure document has been reviewed, approved, and placed under document control.
- Selected test scripts have been reviewed.
- All test scripts have been executed at least once.
- SCM tools are in place, and all source code is under configuration control.
- Software problem reporting procedures are in place.
- Software validation testing completion criteria have been developed, reviewed, and approved.

This list should be supplemented with any additional project-specific criteria.

9.2.3.4 Test execution (formal validation)

After the software validation readiness review has been held and project management has determined that the criteria have been met, the formal validation testing phase begins. At this point in the project, software changes are restricted to changes required to fix bugs. *No new functionality can be added.*

During the formal validation testing phase, the following activities are performed:

- Test scripts are executed and the results recorded.
- Software problem reports (SPRs) are submitted for each test that fails (i.e., the software does not meet requirements).
- SPR tracking is performed and includes the status of all SPRs (open, fixed, verified, deferred, not a bug, etc.)
- Each SPR should identify the modules that need to be changed to fix the bug.
- Baseline change assessment is used to ensure that only those modules that should be changed actually have been changed.
- Informal code reviews (not formal inspections) on changed modules are selectively conducted to ensure that new bugs are not being introduced.
- The time required to find and fix bugs (find/fix cycle) is tracked.
- Regression testing is performed:

- Use the complexity measures discussed in Chapter 7 to help determine which modules may need additional testing.
- Use your judgment in deciding which tests need to be rerun.
- Use your knowledge of software design and past history to decide what tests need to be rerun.

- Track test status (passed, failed, not run, etc.).
- Record cumulative test time (cumulative hours of actual testing) for software reliability growth tracking (described in Chapter 11).

9.2.3.5   Test completion criteria

A key element of the software validation test plan is the criteria that must be met to complete validation testing. It is important that the completion criteria be defined, reviewed, and approved early in the process.

Examples of completion criteria follow.

- All test scripts have been executed.
- All SPRs have been satisfactorily resolved (fixed, deferred to a later release, not a bug, etc.). All parties must agree to the resolution. This could be defined such that all high-priority (P1) bugs must be fixed, priority 2 (P2) bugs are handled on a case-by-case basis, and so on.
- All changes made as a result of SPRs have been tested.
- All documentation associated with the software (SRS, SDD, test documents, etc.) have been updated to reflect changes made during validation testing.
- The test report has been reviewed and approved.

The test report documents the results of the formal software validation testing process. An sample test report is included in Appendix H. Information that is typically in the test report includes the following:

- A completed copy of each test script with evidence that the script was executed (i.e., signature of person who performed testing);
- A copy of each SPR showing resolution;
- A list of open or unresolved SPRs;
- Identification of SPRs found in each baseline along with total number of SPRs in each baseline (perhaps with a bar chart to illustrate the trend);

- The regression tests executed in each baseline.

9.3 Summary

The main points of this chapter are the following:

- Unfortunately, unit testing is often viewed as a debugging activity rather than a testing activity.
- There are several different approaches to integration testing.
- Validation testing is effective only if the SRS is used as the basis for developing both the tests and the software.
- Validation testing is a complex activity that needs to be planned and managed.
- Informal validation testing occurs in parallel with software development.
- Criteria that must be met to start formal validation testing should be defined and included in the software validation test plan.
- Criteria that must be met to complete formal validation testing should be defined and included in the software validation test plan.

Finding bugs as a result of testing is a random activity. The likelihood of finding an as yet undiscovered bug is directly related to the specific tests that are run. Testing, to be effective, must be performed rigorously and in a controlled environment. Configuration management plays a key role in helping to increase the effectiveness of the testing activity.

REFERENCES

[1] Myers, G. J., *The Art of Software Testing*, New York: Wiley, 1976.

[2] Humphrey, W. S., *Managing the Software Process*, Reading, MA: Addison-Wesley, 1989.

[3] ANSI/IEEE Standard 1012-1986, *IEEE Standard for Software Verification and Validation Plans*, 1986, IEEE, Inc., 345 East 47th Street, NY, NY 10017.

[4] ANSI/IEEE Guide 1059-1994, *IEEE Guide for Software Verification and Validation Plans*, 1994, IEEE, Inc., 345 East 47th Street, NY, NY 10017.

[5] Draft International Standard ISO/IEC-12207-1995, *Information Technology Software—Life Cycle Processes*, August 1995.

[6] IEEE Standard 729-1983, *IEEE Standard Glossary of Software Engineering Terminology*, 1983, IEEE, Inc., 345 East 47th Street, NY, NY 10017.

[7] ANSI/IEEE Standard 1008-1987, *IEEE Standard for Software Unit Testing*, 1986, IEEE, Inc., 345 East 47th Street, NY, NY 10017.

[8] Pressman, R., *Software Engineering: A Practitioner's Approach*, 3rd Ed., New York: McGraw-Hill, 1992.

[9] ANSI/IEEE Standard 829-1983, *IEEE Standard for Software Test Documentation*, 1983, IEEE, Inc., 345 East 47th Street, NY, NY 10017.

Chapter 10

Software validation metrics

S OFTWARE VALIDATION activities are critical to the successful launch of a
new product. An effective software validation effort can lead to lower
support costs, more satisfied customers, and more efficient use of scarce
software engineering resources (as a result of fewer bugs, less time is required
for bug fixing; therefore, more time is available to work on the next product).

On the other hand, an unsuccessful software validation effort can result in
the release of a product that has a significant number of bugs. Customers will
be dissatisfied with the product (especially if a competitor's product has significantly fewer bugs), and scarce software engineering and customer support
resources will be spending most of their time fixing bugs and dealing with irate
customers—not a pretty picture.

To help ensure that software validation activities are as effective as possible,
the process must be planned and managed. On any given software development
project, you should be able to answer the following software validation testing
questions:

- How many tests do we need?
- What resources are needed to develop the required tests?
- How much time is required to execute the tests?
- How much time is required to find bugs, fix them, and verify that they have been fixed?
- How much time has been spent actually testing the product?
- How much of the code is being exercised?
- Are we testing all of the product's features?
- How many defects have been detected in each software baseline?

This chapter discusses each of these questions and describes how the answers can be used to improve the effectiveness of software validation activities.

10.1 Time measures

10.1.1 Test estimates

The question, "How many tests do we need?" can have a significant impact on the cost and schedule of a given project. Humphrey observed that, "While there is no magic way to select a sufficient set of practical tests, the objective is to test reasonably completely all valid classes for normal operation and to exhaustively test unusual behavior and illegal conditions" [1].

The question of how many tests are needed must be answered early on so adequate resources (people and equipment) can be arranged and accurate and realistic schedules developed.

The test estimate measure reflects the number of tests needed based on factors such as the following:

- Features and functions defined in the SRS and related documents;
- ALAC testing;
- Achieving a test coverage goal;
- Achieving a software reliability goal.

Test estimates should be based on and tied to specific sections of the SRS and other related documents. Starting with the SRS, review each requirement and, based on past experience, estimate the number of tests needed to determine whether the software has met the requirement. In addition to tests that are tied directly to the SRS, you should also develop a reasonable number of ALAC tests that are representative of customer use of the product.

As discussed in Chapter 9, ALAC tests allow you to focus on finding those bugs that customers are most likely to find. Acting like a customer also means developing tests that [2]:

- Do it wrong;
- Use wrong or illegal combinations of input;
- Do not do enough;
- Do nothing;
- Do too much.

The test estimate should also reflect the complexity of tests as well as manual versus automated tests. Manual tests are tests that require a person to execute the test. Automated tests are developed like manual tests but can be executed repeatedly under computer control. Automated tests are particularly well suited for testing user interfaces. Several excellent automated test tools (generally referred to as capture/playback tools) are available. (Refer to further information at the end of this chapter.)

Developing tests should be viewed as an investment. The time and effort required to identify, write, and debug a test can be more than recouped based on the costs required to find and fix bugs once a product has been released. Building up a large suite of good regression tests is like having money in the bank.

Like most estimating tasks, the first time you make a test estimate, you may find that your estimate and the actual number of tests developed are very different. At the end of a project, do a postmortem and understand why there was a discrepancy. Learn from past experience, and your estimates will continually get better.

The test estimate metric is measured in units that are the number of tests to be written. To improve your ability to accurately estimate the magnitude of the software validation testing task, use this measure to compare the estimated number of tests to the actual number written.

10.1.2 Test development time

Once you have made an estimate of the number of tests required, the next question is, "How much effort is needed to develop the required tests?"

The test development time includes the time required to develop a first draft of a test, to debug the test, and to revise the test

The test development time metric should reflect the relative complexity of tests as well as manual versus automated tests.

The units of the test development time metric are person-hours per test. To improve your ability to accurately estimate the magnitude of the validation testing task, use this measure to compare the estimated time required to develop, debug, and revise tests with the actual time required.

Once you have estimated the number of tests required and the test development time, you can then develop a realistic schedule for the software validation test development activity.

10.1.3   Test execution time

The next question to answer is, "How much time is required to execute the tests?"

The test execution time metric is an estimate of the time required to execute tests. Like the two previous metrics, test execution time should reflect the complexity of the tests as well as manual versus automated tests. You can develop an average execution time for automated tests, manual tests, complex tests, and simple tests. Use these averages to determine the amount of time required to execute all the tests.

This estimate does not include time for regression testing required to verify bug fixes made during software validation testing. As a rule of thumb, allow an additional 25% to 50% of the total test execution time for regression testing, depending on factors such as inspections held, amount of new code versus reused or modified code, amount of unit and integration testing performed, and so on.

The units of the test execution time metric are person-hours per test. To improve your ability to accurately estimate the magnitude of the validation testing task, use this measure to compare the estimated time required to execute tests with the actual time required.

Use the test execution time estimate with the test estimate and the number of resources available (people and equipment) to develop the software validation testing schedule. Remember to allow time for regression testing.

10.1.4   Find/fix cycle time

The find/fix cycle time answers the question, "How much time is required to find bugs, fix them, and verify that they have been fixed?" As was illustrated in

Figure 4.4, this measure includes the time required to peform the following activities:

- Find a potential bug by executing a test;
- Submit a problem report to the software engineering group;
- Investigate the problem report;
- Determine corrective action;
- Perform root cause analysis;
- Test the correction locally;
- Conduct a mini-code inspection on changed modules;
- Incorporate corrective action into a new baseline;
- Release new the baseline to the software validation team;
- Perform regression testing to verify that the reported problem has been fixed and that the fix has not introduced new problems.

The units of the find/fix cycle time metric are person-hours per SPR. Use this measure to help justify increasing the amount of effort spent on prevention and detection activities and to compute the cost of quality. This measure represents activities that fall into the nonconformance category.

10.1.5 Cumulative test time

This metric answers the question, "How much time has been spent actually using and testing the system?" This measure represents the cumulative testing time for all validation testing activities.

Cumulative test time metric units are test hours. Use this measure to compute software reliability growth (discussed in Chapter 11).

10.2 Test coverage metrics

10.2.1 Code coverage

The test coverage metric answers the question, "How much of the code is being exercised?" Two types of coverage metrics can be used:

- *Segment coverage:* Units are the percentage of segments hit;
- *Call-pair coverage:* Units are the percentage of call pairs hit.

The test coverage measures are useful during all phases of testing. They help drive the development of additional tests to ensure that as much code as possible is exercised.

10.2.1.1 Segment coverage

A segment is a set of program statements that are executed unconditionally or executed conditionally based on the value of some logical expression or predicate in the program. Basic facts regarding segments and segment coverage are:

- Every (executable) statement is in some segment.
- A segment corresponds to an edge in a program's directed graph, as illustrated in Figure 10.1.
- Segment coverage is especially useful during unit and integration testing.
- Segment coverage is cumulative.
- A goal of 85% is a practical coverage value.

10.2.1.2 Call Pairs

A call pair is an interface whereby one module invokes another. Call-pair coverage is especially useful during integration testing to ensure that all module interfaces are exercised. A goal of 100% is a practical coverage value.

Because call-pair coverage is less detailed than segment coverage, it is more suitable for large systems.

10.2.2 Requirements coverage

The requirements coverage metric answers the question, "Are we testing all of the system's features?" An RTM, similar to that shown in Table 10.1, is used to trace requirements (in the SRS) to tests.

The unit for the requirements coverage metric is the percentage of requirements covered by at least one test.

The requirements coverage metric is used to ensure that all features are covered by at least one test. The RTM is also useful for test estimates and for identifying tests that need to be changed when requirements change.

10.3 Quality metric

The defect density is a quality metric that answers the question, "How many defects have been detected in each software baseline?" During software

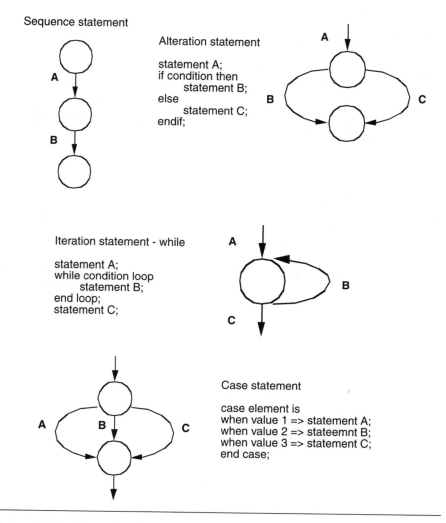

Sequence statement

Alteration statement

statement A;
if condition then
        statement B;
else
        statement C;
endif;

Iteration statement - while

statement A;
while condition loop
        statement B;
end loop;
statement C;

Case statement

case element is
when value 1 => statement A;
when value 2 => stateemnt B;
when value 3 => statement C;
end case;

Figure 10.1   Directed graphs.

validation, new baselines are built to reflect bug fixes resulting from bugs found by software validation testing. The number of bugs found in each baseline is representative of the overall improvement in quality and usually is depicted as a bar chart, as illustrated in Figure 10.2.

The unit of the defect density metric is the number of SPRs per baseline. This measure can be used to help make decisions regarding process improvements, additional regression testing, and release of the system for shipment to customers.

Table 10.1   Example of an RTM

Requirement (SRS)	Design (SDD)	Code (Modules)	Tests (Test Procedure)	Notes
4.1.2: User interface	8.2.2: Entering data	userin.c	Test scripts #102, 103, 104	Range checking of user entered data
4.1.4: Calculation accuracy and precision	5.6.3: Calculations	calc.c	Test scripts #405, 506, 660	Calculation accuracy and precision
4.1.5: Performance	4.2.3: Performance	All	Test scripts #221, 210–220	Performance measured with typical system loading
4.1.6: Data storage	4.4.1: Database	datab.c	Test scripts #321, 332	Empty and full conditions checked

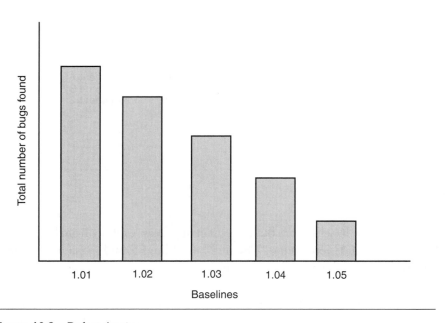

Figure 10.2   Defect density.

10.4 Summary

Measures related to the software validation testing activity are essential for improving the effectiveness of this activity. A good estimate of the software validation testing task increases the likelihood that the company's product will be released on time and with an acceptable level of quality.

REFERENCES

[1]   Humphrey, W. S., *Managing the Software Process*, Reading, MA: Addison-Wesley, 1989.

[2]   Beizer, B., *Software Testing Techniques*, New York: Van Nostrand Reinhold, 1983.

Further information

Information on automated test tools can be found in Brian Marick's list published periodically in the Usenet discussion group: comp.software.testing .

Chapter 11

Software reliability growth

MORE OFTEN THAN NOT, software is delivered later than planned. When the software finally is delivered, it usually has less functionality than the customer expected, and the functionality that is delivered usually is buggy.

This problem frequently can be traced to the fact that management and customers may have different perspectives on issues related to software quality. When asked about the quality of their product, management may say, "The software should be fault free." While a noble statement, it is one that is not within reach for most software companies. Customers, on the other hand, have a very different perspective, as illustrated by this statement: "I expect software to operate for x hours per week without any downtime." Clearly, customers realize it is unreasonable to expect software to be fault free. What the customer is expressing is a requirement for an expected level of reliability, "which is probably the most important of the characteristics inherent in the concept of 'software quality'" [1].

Three key questions are frequently asked during the last few weeks prior to software being released.

- Is this version of software ready for release (however you define *ready*)?
- How much additional effort is required to release software?
- When will the software be ready for release?

The purpose of this chapter is to help answer these questions by developing a software reliability growth model. Such a model enables organizations to develop a reliability goal and to track progress toward that goal by collecting data during software validation testing and, as a result, providing answers to those three questions.

11.1 Definitions

Before we begin the discussion of software reliability growth modeling, we need to define a few key terms. These are listed in Table 11.1.

Table 11.1   Software Reliability Growth Definitions

Software reliability	The probability of failure-free operation of a computer program for a specified period of time operating in a specified environment [1]
Reliability growth	The improvement in software reliability that results from correcting faults in the software [2]
Software availability	The expected fraction of time during which the software functions acceptably [1]
Fault	A defect (or bug) in the software that causes a software failure
Failure	A departure of the software's operation from user requirements
Failure intensity	The number of failures occurring in a given time period
Mean time to failure (MTTF)	The average value of the next failure interval

11.2 The test-analyze-fix process

Software reliability growth changes as a result of the test-analyze-fix process. This process was illustrated by the defect removal cycles shown in Figures 4.4 and 4.5.

Testing stimulates the occurrence of failures. As each failure is detected, a root cause analysis is performed. Corrective action is applied that corrects the immediate problem. Preventive action, based on the root cause analysis, prevents the same failure mode from occurring again and reduces the rate of failure mode occurrence.

Thus, the way to achieve software reliability growth is by using testing to identify failures and then performing root cause analysis, which results in a reduction in the occurrence of the specific failure mode.

11.3 Reliability growth modeling

Modeling software reliability growth can help answer the three questions posed at the beginning of this chapter. By having a robust model of how the reliability of the software changes over time, management can make decisions regarding testing, release, and expected level of support required after release.

As Musa [1] observed:

> To model software reliability one must first consider the principal factors that affect it: fault introduction, fault removal, and the environment. Fault introduction depends primarily on the characteristics of the developed code...and the development process characteristics. The most significant code characteristic is size. Development process characteristics include engineering technologies and tools used and the level of expertise of personnel. ...Fault removal depends on time, operational profile, and the quality of the repair activity. The environment directly depends on the operational profile. Since some of the foregoing factors are probabilistic in nature and operate over time, software reliability models are generally distinguished from each other in general terms by the nature of the variation of the random process with time.

11.3.1   The objectives of modeling

The application of modeling techniques to measure software reliability can help achieve the following objectives:

- To measure and predict software reliability in terms of MTTF;
- To determine the optimal time to stop testing and release the software;
- To provide data for making tradeoffs between test time, reliability, cost, and performance goals;
- To define realistic software reliability goals.

Many software organizations are making these decisions today using the GF ("gut feel") model. As observed by Musa [1], a good software reliability model has several important characteristics:

- It predicts future failure behavior.
- It computes meaningful results.
- It is simple, widely applicable, and based on sound assumptions.

By properly applying a software reliability growth model, we can get answers to the three questions posed at the beginning of this chapter.

11.3.2   Types of models

As illustrated in Figure 11.1, two classes of models can be applied. Empirical models involve fitting a curve to reliability growth data on a log-log scale. Mathematical models are based on modeling the reliability growth as a stochastic process. Both classes of models have advantages and disadvantages. (A complete discussion of the different classes of models and other relevant topics can be found in Musa [1] and the *IEEE Guide for the Use of IEEE Standard Dictionary of Measures to Produce Reliable Software* [3].)

Because software reliability is a function of fault introduction, fault removal, and the environment, the discovery of a new fault is a random event. As a result, we can use data analysis and prediction models. More specifically, we can use models that operate in the time and data domains. Such models typically are easier to use than many of the other types of models and can produce results that are just as accurate.

Table 11.2 gives a list of time and data domain models.

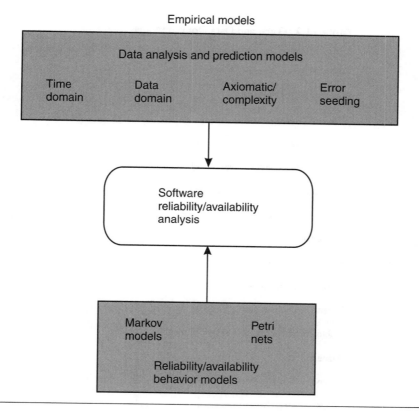

Empirical models

Figure 11.1   Types of models.

11.3.3   Model assumptions

All models make assumptions. The process of selecting a model has much to do with the assumptions that models make.

There are three types of assumptions:

- Universal assumptions, which are made by all models, for example:
  - Times between failures are independent.
  - Testing is representative of actual use.
  - Faults are of similar severity.
  - Time is used as basis of failure rate.

- Criteria assumptions, which are made by some models, for example:
  - The number of potential faults is fixed and finite.
  - Detected faults are fixed immediately.

Table 11.2   Time and Data Domain Models

Jelinski-Moranda de-eutrophication model*

Shooman exponential model

Schick-Wolverton model*

Goel-Okumoto nonhomogeneous Poisson process*

Goel generalized nonhomogeneous Poisson process

Littlewood Bayesian debugging model

Brooks-Motley model*

Goel-Okumoto imperfect debugging model

Musa execution time model

Lipow's extension model

Generalized Poisson model*

Rushforth, Staffanson, and Crawford model

Duane model

Moranda geometric model

Littlewood-Veral Bayesian reliability growth model

Moranda geometric progression model

Schneidewind model

Littlewood semi-Markov model

Musa-Okumoto logarithmic Poisson execution time model

Thompson-Chelson Bayesian reliability model

---

* Additional information is included in Appendix J.

- Individual fault occurrence times are recorded (vs. fault occurrences grouped by time intervals).

New faults can be introduced as a result of fixing existing faults.

- Particular assumptions, which are made by individual models, for example:

- There is a fixed number of errors in the code.
- No new errors are introduced through the bug fixing process.
- The program size is constant (no new code is being added).
- The detection of errors is an independent process.
- The testing is performed in a manner that is similar to intended usage.
- The error detection rate is proportional to the number of errors remaining in the code.

In addition to assumptions, each model also has specific data requirements. That is, you may need to collect specific information that is needed for the model. Model assumptions and data requirements usually are clearly defined in the description of the model.

11.3.4 The model selection process

Consider the following factors before selecting a particular model to use.

- There is no one best model.
- Each model has advantages and disadvantages.
- Match the model's assumptions to your software development process.
- Use more than one model to validate your results.
- Models use data based on actual faults obtained as a result of software validation testing.

Based on these considerations, a general process for selecting a model can be described.

1. Use criteria assumptions to select a group of candidate models.
2. Compare each model's particular assumptions with your software development process and narrow the list of candidates to two or three.
3. Identify the data requirements for each selected model and determine how to collect the data.
4. Once the data have been collected, apply the models to the data.
5. Perform a goodness-of-fit test and determine if each model meets your goodness-of fit-criteria.
6. Rank the models based on the goodness-of-fit criteria.

11.3.5   Applying the selected model

After a model has been selected, the next step in the process is to collect the required data. The data usually is collected during the software validation testing phase of a project. For example, say you have chosen the Duane model. You would need to collect the cumulative testing time and the time to each fault. Collection of this information should be automated, if possible. If that is not possible, use lab notebooks to record testing time and time to each fault.

As faults are detected during the software validation process, the information is entered into the model. Periodically, a graph similar to that shown in Figure 11.2 can be created, showing progress toward a reliability goal. The reliability goal can be expressed as, for example, the number of faults found by customers that require immediate correction.

Once a model has been selected and applied, the results produced from the model need to be validated against actual experience. That requires collection of actual failure data once the product is released and a comparison of the actual data to those predicted by the model.

11.3.6   Reliability Modeling Tools

The Statistical Modeling and Estimation of Reliability Functions for Software (SMERFS) [4] contains a collection of several reliability models, including:

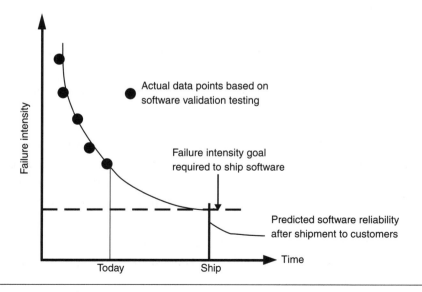

Figure 11.2   Software reliability growth model.

- The Littlewood-Veral Bayesian model;
- The Musa execution time model;
- The geometric model*;
- The nonhomogeneous Poisson model for execution time data;
- The Musa logarithmic Poisson execution time model;
- The generalized Poisson model for interval data;
- The nonhomogeneous Poisson model for interval data;
- The Brooks-Motley discrete software reliability model*;
- The Schneidewind maximum likelihood model;
- The Yamada S-shaped reliability growth model.

SMERFS is available for minimal cost from William H. Farr, Naval Surface Warfare Center, Dahlgren, VA 22448-5000. An example of a SMERFS model is shown in Table 11.3.

11.4 Summary

Software reliability growth modeling provides management with another piece of quantitative data to use in making key decisions regarding product quality. These data can be extremely helpful in determining when to stop testing and release a product.

The key points regarding software reliability growth are the following:

- There are many software reliability models.
- Accuracy of models varies widely.
- Significant differences result from using different models.
- There is no one best model
- It is possible to obtain an accurate reliability prediction using these models if the selection process is followed.
- Try as many models as possible and select the one (or ones) that provides the "best" results.

---

*   Additional information included in Appendix J.

Table 11.3 Example of a SMERFS Model

Model	Assumptions	Data Requirements
Generalized Poisson model	The expected number of errors occurring in any time interval is proportional to the error content at the time of testing and to some function of the amount of time spent testing. All errors are equally likely to occur and are independent of each other. Each error is of the same order of severity as any other error. The software is tested in a manner similar to intended usage. The errors are corrected at the ends of testing intervals without introduction of new errors into the program. Errors discovered in one testing interval can be corrected in others; the only restriction is that corrections be made at the end of an interval.	The length (time) of each testing interval The number of errors corrected at the end of each testing interval The number of errors discovered in each testing interval

- Data collection is usually the most difficult problem.
- Software reliability growth modeling, like anything else, needs to be subject to continuous process improvement.

REFERENCES

[1] Musa, J. D., A. Iannino, and K. Okumoto, *Software Reliability Measurement, Prediction, and Application*, New York: McGraw-Hill, 1987.

[2] ANSI/IEEE Standard 729-1983, *IEEE Standard Glossary of Software Engineering Terminology*, 1983, IEEE, Inc., 345 East 47th Street, NY, NY 10017.

[3] IEEE Standard 982.2-1988, *IEEE Guide for the Use of IEEE Standard Dictionary of Measures to Produce Reliable Software*, 1988, IEEE, Inc., 345 East 47th Street, NY, NY 10017.

[4] Farr, W. H., *Statistical Modeling and Estimation of Reliability Functions for Software (SMERFS) Library Access Guide*, NAVSWC TR-84-371, Rev. 2, March 1991.

Appendix A

Inspection roles and responsibilities

ONE OF THE MOST important aspects of the inspection process is that team members play specific roles. For the inspection process to be successful, it is essential that each team member know the role he or she is to play and the responsibilities of that role. It is expected that people eventually will play all the different roles as the inspection process becomes part of a company's culture.

A.1 Roles

An inspection team consists of three to six people who play the following roles:

- Moderator;
- Producer;
- Reader;
- Recorder (optional);

- Inspector.

The producer's immediate supervisor or manager, while not directly involved in the inspection process, does play a role in the inspection process. The manager's role and responsibilities are to participate in the decision of what to inspect; include inspections on project schedules; allocate resources for inspections; support inspection training; participate in the selection of moderators; and support the moderator in getting rework completed.

A.2 Responsibilities

Each inspection team member has specific responsibilities.

A.2.1 Moderator

The moderator is a key player in the inspection process. Selection of the moderator is crucial to the success of the inspection process. A good moderator will ensure that the inspection team is selected appropriately, is trained in the inspection process, is adequately prepared for the inspection, and abides by the guidelines for inspection meetings.

Selection of the moderator is, therefore, very important. The moderator is usually selected from a small group of senior people who have had prior experience as moderators and who are well respected for their technical skills as well as their people management skills.

The moderator must be able to:

- Understand the information being inspected;
- Lead the team in an effective discussion;
- Mediate disputes;
- Recognize key issues and keep the team focused on them;
- Maintain an unbiased view of the information being inspected;
- Assign responsibilities appropriately.

The specific responsibilities of the moderator are:

- To select inspection team members;
- To ensure that team members can devote sufficient time to the inspection and are not involved in other activities that could impair their ability to spend the required amount of time preparing for the inspection;

- To ensure that the manager of the person whose work is being inspected is aware of the inspection;
- To schedule the inspection meeting and make the necessary logistical arrangements for conference rooms, review materials, and so on;
- To ensure that the inspection team is adequately prepared to conduct the inspection or, if the team is not prepared, to postpone the inspection meeting;
- To ensure that the inspection meeting is conducted in an orderly and efficient manner, starting promptly and ending on time;
- To ensure that all problems found during the inspection meeting are properly documented;
- To track each problem identified to closure;
- To prepare and distribute meeting minutes within two working days after the inspection meeting.

The moderator is usually selected by the producer and the producer's manager.

A.2.2 Producer

The producer is the person who prepared the information or work product that is to be inspected. Inspections are conducted for the benefit of the producer. The reward for the other inspection team members is the satisfaction gained from helping a peer improve the quality of the company's product. There is an implied understanding that they will be helped in return.

The producer's responsibilities are:

- To ensure that the work product to be inspected is ready for inspection;
- To make required information available on time;
- To support the moderator in making meeting arrangements, providing copies of materials, and helping to establish schedules for any required corrective action;
- To promptly resolve all problems identified by the inspection team;
- To remain objective and avoid becoming defensive.

The producer attends the inspection meeting to clarify any issues that are not clear to the inspectors. The producer does not justify why he or she developed the work product a certain way. Remember that the objective of the inspection is to determine if the work product, as it presently exists, meets established requirements.

A.2.3 Reader

The reader is responsible for paraphrasing portions of the work product being inspected so the inspection team can focus on small chunks of information. This helps divert attention away from the producer and toward the product. The reader is also an inspector and has the same responsibilities as inspectors.

The additional responsibilities of the reader are:

- To be thoroughly familiar with the work product being inspected;
- To identify logical chunks of information and to be able to paraphrase the information in each chunk, thereby allowing the moderator to keep the team focused on one chunk at a time;
- To support the moderator.

A.2.4 Inspectors

Inspectors are selected based on their knowledge and familiarity with the work product being inspected. Inspectors are also selected to represent a cross-section of skills. For example, at a code inspection, inspectors representing software engineering, marketing, and manufacturing may be selected. Inspectors are expected to devote the necessary time and effort to become thoroughly familiar with the work product. Their role is to look for discrepancies between the work product and the documentation and standards against which the work product is being inspected. Each inspector should expect that, at some future date, he or she will be in the role of the producer.

The inspector's responsibilities are:

- To be thoroughly familiar with the work product being inspected as well as the documents and standards against which the work product is being inspected;
- To identify discrepancies between the work product and the documentation and standards;
- To focus on identifying problems, not solving them;
- To remain objective;
- To criticize the product, not the producer;
- To support the moderator.

A.2.5 Recorder (optional role)

Recording information during an inspection can be a time-consuming task. Rather than burden the moderator with this task, many times a team member acts as the recorder. The recorder captures all issues and problems raised by the team, thus allowing the moderator to focus on leading the discussion. For each issue raised by the team, the recorder captures a complete description of the issue. The recorder is also an inspector and has the same responsibilities as inspectors.

The role of the recorder is optional. Depending on the size and the nature of the inspection, the moderator may assume the responsibilities of recorder.

The recorder's additional responsibilities are:

- To be thoroughly familiar with the work product being inspected;
- To record all issues raised by the team and ensure that they are recorded correctly;
- To provide additional information as requested by the moderator;
- To support the moderator.

A.2.6 Manager

The manager's role and responsibilities are:

- To help decide what to inspect;
- To include inspections in project schedules;
- To allocate resources for inspections;
- To support inspection training;
- To participate in the selection of moderators;
- To support the moderator in completing any required rework.

Appendix B

A sample inspection process

THE SECOND OF the five basic elements of the inspection process is a documented process for conducting inspections. A documented process provides the basis for performing inspections in a manner such that everyone can understand the process and how they can contribute to its success. Having a written process also provides the basic materials required for training.

The inspection process has five steps:

1. Planning;
2. Overview meeting (optional);
3. Preparation;
4. Inspection meeting;
5. Follow-up.

This appendix discusses these steps in detail. For each step, the following information is included:

- *Objectives:* the purpose of the step;
- *Entry criteria:* the conditions that must be met to begin the step;
- *Activities:* the activities that occur as part of the step;
- *Exit criteria:* the conditions that must be met to complete the step;
- *Metrics:* the product and process data that should be collected.

B.1 Planning

B.1.1 Objectives

- To determine which work products need to be inspected;
- To determine if a work product that needs to be inspected is ready to be inspected;
- To identify the inspection team;
- To determine if an overview meeting is needed;
- To schedule the optional overview meeting and the inspection meeting.

B.1.2 Entry criteria

The manager and the producer identify the work product to be inspected. Examples of work products are SRS, SDD, source code, and test procedures.

B.1.3 Activities

- Identify the work product to be inspected and determine if the work product is ready to be inspected (refer to Table 5.2).
- Select the moderator. The producer and the producer's manager select the moderator for the inspection.
- Identify inspection team members. Once the moderator has been selected and has accepted the assignment, the moderator and the producer determine the makeup of the inspection team. The nature of the work product being inspected determines if inspectors from other

engineering disciplines are needed. For example, if the work product is communications software that interfaces with hardware, the engineer who designed the hardware should be on the team. A representative from the software QA group is invited to all inspection meetings. The minimum number of people required for an inspection is three (moderator, producer, and one inspector). The maximum number of people for an inspection should be limited to six or seven.

- The moderator ensures that all inspection team members have had inspection process training.

- The moderator obtains a commitment from each team member to participate. This commitment means the person agrees to spend the time required to perform his or her assigned role on the team. In some cases, approval from the team member's supervisor or manager may be required.

- The moderator and the producer decide if an overview meeting is required based on the inspection team's familiarity with the work product being inspected, the amount and complexity of information the team must review to be prepared for the inspection, and the complexity of the work product being inspected.

- The moderator schedules meetings and distributes review materials. The moderator communicates the date, time, and location of the meetings to the inspection team. If an overview meeting is held, the moderator can distribute the review materials at that meeting.

- The moderator and the producer identify the review materials required for the inspection (see Chapter 5). The moderator ensures that the review materials are distributed (and received) at least five working days before the inspection meeting, so the inspection team has sufficient time to prepare for the inspection.

- Inspection meetings should be limited to two hours in duration. Studies have shown that the effectiveness of the inspection diminishes after two hours. Inspection meetings also should be limited to two per day. Use the following guideline to estimate the amount of material that can be inspected in two hours:

  - Work product is a document: 10 to 20 pages per hour;
  - Work product is code: 100 to 200 source statements per hour (based on C).

B.1.4 Exit criteria

The planning phase is complete when the following tasks have been accomplished:

- The inspection team has been selected and trained and its members are committed.
- Review materials have been identified and distributed at least five working days in advance.
- An overview meeting, if required, has been scheduled.
- The inspection meeting has been scheduled.

B.1.5 Metrics

The process metric that should be recorded during the planning phase is the time spent by each person in the planning phase measured in person-hours.

B.2 Overview meeting (optional)

B.2.1 Objective

The objective of the overview meeting is to educate the inspection team on the work product being inspected and to discuss the review materials.

B.2.2 Entry criteria

- The work product is ready to be inspected (see Chapter 5).
- The producer has prepared an overview of the work product and the review materials.
- The review materials are ready to be distributed.

B.2.3 Activities

- The moderator distributes the work product and the review materials.
- The producer describes the information contained in the review materials and the relationship to the work product.
- The producer provides the context for the work product and how the work product fits into the big picture.

- Team members ask questions to facilitate their understanding of the work product and the information in the review materials.

B.2.4 Exit criteria

The overview meeting has been held and all questions have been resolved.

B.2.5 Metrics

- Preparation time by the producer;
- Duration of the overview meeting.
- The moderator multiplies the number of participants by the meeting duration and enters that number in the appropriate place on the Inspection Process Summary Report (see Appendix C). The measure is person-hours.

B.3 Preparation

B.3.1 Objective

To prepare for the inspection meeting by critically reviewing the review materials and the work product.

B.3.2 Entry criteria

- The work product is ready to be inspected.
- The overview meeting, if required, has been held.
- The review materials and the work product have been distributed to the inspection team members.

B.3.3 Activities

B.3.3.1 Inspectors

- Review prompting checklists and internal standards and conventions before reviewing work product to create mental list of things to look for;
- Become very familiar with review materials and work product;

- Review the work product against the review materials, and record any discrepancies on an Inspection Problem Report form (see Appendix C);
- Keep track of preparation time and bring that information to the meeting.

B.3.3.2 Reader

- Performs same activities as inspectors;
- Breaks down the work products into chunks and then paraphrases or summarizes those chunks in his or her own words.
- Keeps track of preparation time and brings that information to the meeting.

B.3.4 Exit criteria

Each team member is prepared for the inspection meeting.

B.3.5 Metrics

Preparation time, measured in person-hours.

B.4 Inspection meeting

B.4.1 Objective

The objective of the inspection meeting is to identify errors and defects in the work product being inspected.

B.4.2 Entry criteria

The inspection team members have completed the required preparation.

B.4.3 Activities

- The moderator calls the meeting to order promptly.
- The moderator reviews the ground rules for the meeting: (1) The objective of the inspection meeting is to find problems, not solve them; (2) criticism is to be focused on the product, not the producer; (3) the producer is present to clarify, not justify; and (4) the meeting duration is set at two hours.

- The moderator determines if the inspectors are prepared. One way to determine if the team is prepared is to ask each inspector to write down how much time he or she spent preparing for the meeting. If, in the moderator's opinion, the team is not adequately prepared, the moderator postpones the meeting.

- If the moderator is satisfied that the team is adequately prepared, the inspection begins. The reader starts by paraphrasing the first chunk of information from the work product.

- The moderator then goes around the table and solicits any potential errors or defects from the team. Each potential error or defect is discussed, and the team reaches consensus as to whether a potential problem should be recorded as an error or a defect.

- Each potential problem is recorded on an Inspection Problem Report form for consistency.

- The producer can provide clarification but not justification.

- The recorder ensures that the information entered on the Inspection Problem Report forms is complete and accurate and reflects any team discussions and clarifications.

- After the reader has completed paraphrasing the entire work product, the moderator asks the recorder to read back all the Inspection Problem Report forms to ensure they were recorded correctly.

- The team decides if the severity of the problems found warrants another inspection or if the moderator can review the corrective action without another inspection meeting.

- The recorder records the meeting duration information on the Inspection Process Summary Report form (see Appendix C).

- If another meeting is required, the moderator schedules it.

- The moderator adjourns the meeting.

B.4.4 Exit criteria

- The inspection meeting has been held.

- Errors and defects identified at the meeting are documented on the Inspection Problem Report forms

- The Inspection Process Summary Report form has been completed.

- The meeting minutes are published and distributed within two working days after the inspection meeting.

B.4.5 Metrics

- Time spent by each team member during the inspection meeting, measured in person-hours;
- Size of work product being inspected, measured in number of pages (for documents) or KLOCs (for code);
- Number of problems identified.

B.5 Follow-up

B.5.1 Objective

To ensure that corrective action has been taken to correct problems found during an inspection.

B.5.2 Entry criteria

The producer has completed the necessary rework.

B.5.3 Activities

- The producer and the moderator agree on the schedule for completing corrective action.
- The producer resolves the problems identified by the inspection team.
- When all rework has been completed, the moderator inspects the rework and records the resolution of each problem on the Inspection Problem Report form or reschedules a follow-up inspection meeting, as determined by the team.

B.5.4 Exit criteria

- All reported problems have been corrected and reviewed by the moderator.
- The moderator completes the rework section of the Inspection Problem Report form.

- The moderator issues a follow-up report informing inspection team members of the completed rework.

B.5.5 Metrics

- The producer records the time spent in rework for each problem, measured in person-hours.
- The moderator records the elapsed calendar time from when the inspection meeting was held to completion of follow-up, measured in days.

Appendix C

Inspection process forms

Tables C.1 and C.2 display the Inspection Problem Report Form and the Inspection Process Summary Report, respectively.

Table C.1   The Inspection Problem Report Form

INSPECTION PROBLEM REPORT	Report No. _____

Inspector

Item Information: Date _____

Item inspected: _____   Inspector: _____

Defect Description: Defect location: _____
_____
_____
_____

Recorder

Meeting Decisions:

❑ Accepted-Planned Resolution dtae: _____
❑ Duplicate of Problem Report No. _____
❑ Rejected-Reason: _____
❑ Deferred-Reason: _____

Impact:	Category:	Type:	Origin:
❑ Local	❑ Missing	❑ Procedure/logic	❑ Requirements
❑ External	❑ Wrong	❑ Interface	❑ Code
	❑ Extra	❑ Data definition	❑ Design
	❑ Unclear	❑ Documentation	❑ Test
	❑ Suggestion	❑ Other: _____	❑ Other: _____

Producer

Resolution: Date: _____

Description: _____
_____
_____
_____ _____

Items changed: _____
_____
_____

Verifier

Verification: Date: _____

Verified by: _____

Items checked: _____
_____

Comments: _____

Table C.2   The Inspection Process Summary Report

INSPECTION PROCESS SUMMARY REPORT

Inspection Information:
Moderator: _____

Inspection Meeting date: _____

Product Information:

Item Identification _____
_____

Errors detected: _____ errors
(Total problems caused by activities in the
process which led to this inspection)

Item size: _____ KLOC or pages
(Code inspection units: thousand lines
non-commented source code.
Document inspection units: pages)

Defects detected: _____ defects
(Total problem caused by activities prior to
the process which led to this inspection)

Resource measures:

Planning: _____ person-hours
(Include time spent by all involved in
planning the inspection)

Preparation: _____ person-hours
(Sum of preparation time for all inspectors

Overview meeting: _____ person-hours
(Meeting duration x number of participants)

Inspection meeting: _____ person-hours
(Meeting duration x number of participants

Meeting Decision:

☐ Item accepted. No errors or defects found.
☐ Meeting rescheduled. Reason: _____
☐ Item rejected. No re-inspection required.
     Rework verification scheduled to be completed by date: _____
☐ Item rejected. Re-inspection required.
     Re-inspection meeting date: _____

Verification of rework:

☐ Accepted. All errors and defects corrected.
☐ Rejected. Additional rework required.
     Additional rework to be completed and verified by date: _____

     Verifier: _____   Date: _____

Appendix D

Inspection checklists

The inspection checklists included in this appendix can help inspectors prepare for an inspection.

D.1 Requirements inspection checklist

1. Do the requirements exhibit a clear distinction between functions and data?
2. Do the requirements define all the information that is to be displayed to the user?
3. Do the requirements address system and user response to error conditions?
4. Is each requirement stated clearly, concisely, and unambiguously?
5. Is each requirement testable?
6. Are there ambiguous or implied requirements?
7. Are there conflicting requirements?
8. Are there areas not addressed in the SRS that need to be?
9. Are performance requirements (such as response time and data storage requirements) stated?
10. If the requirements involve complex decision chains, are they expressed in a form that facilitates comprehension (decision tables, decision trees, etc.)?
11. Are requirements for performing software upgrades specified?
12. Are there requirements that contain an unnecessary level of design detail?
13. Are the real-time constraints specified in sufficient detail?
14. Are the precision and accuracy of calculations specified?
15. Is it possible to develop a thorough set of tests based on the information contained in the SRS? If not, what information is missing?
16. Are assumptions and dependencies clearly stated?
17. Does the document contain all the information called out in the SRS outline?

D.2 Design inspection checklist: high-level design

Assumption: Detailed-level design done using SA/SD methodology

General Requirements and Design

___1.___ Has the review of the design identified problems with the requirements, such as requirements that are missing, ambiguous, extraneous, untestable, or implied?

___2.___ Is the design consistent with the requirements? For example, are there functions that are missing, extraneous, imprecise, ambiguous, or incorrect?

___3.___ Are deviations from the requirements documented and approved?

___4.___ Are all assumptions documented?

___5.___ Have major design decisions been documented?

___6.___ Is the design consistent with those decisions?

___7.___ Does the design adequately address the following issues?

Real-time requirements;
Performance issues (memory and timing);
Spare capacity (CPU and memory) ;
Maintainability;
Understandability;
Database requirements;
Loading and initialization;
Error handling and recovery;
User interface issues;
Software upgrades.

Functional and Interface Specifications

___8.___ Is the Process Spec (P-spec) for each process accurate and complete?

___9.___ Is the P-spec specified in precise, unambiguous terms? Does it clearly describe the required transformations?

___10.___ Are dependencies on other functions, operating system kernel, hardware, etc., identified and documented?

___11.___ Are human factor considerations properly addressed in those functions that provide an user interface?

___12.___ Are design constraints, such as memory and timing budgets, specified where appropriate?

13. Are requirements for error checking, error handling, and recovery specified where needed?

14. Are interfaces consistent with module usage? Missing interfaces? Extra interfaces?

15. Are the interfaces specified to a sufficient level of detail that allows them to be verified?

Conventions

16. Does the design follow the established notation conventions?

D.3 Design inspection checklist: detailed design

Assumption: Detailed-level design done using SA/SD methodology

Requirements Traceability

1. Does the detailed design of this module or interface fulfill its part of the requirements?

2. Has inspection of this module or interface identified problems in the SRS? For example, are any requirements missing, ambiguous, conflicting, untestable, or implied?

3. Does the detailed design of this module or interface meet its high-level design requirements?

4. Has inspection of the detailed design identified problems in the high-level design?

5. Are all functions completely and accurately described in sufficient detail?

6. Are all interfaces completely and accurately described, including keyword or positional parameters, field descriptors, attributes, ranges, and limits?

7. Are the detailed design documents complete and consistent within themselves, i.e., data with logic; all internal data defined; no extraneous data?

Structure and Interfaces

8. At the system and subsystem levels, have all components or modules been identified on a system architecture model?

9. Is the level of decomposition sufficient to identify all modules?

10. Will further decomposition result in identification of more modules?

11. Have all interfaces between system/subsystem elements and modules been clearly and precisely identified?

12. Do successive levels of decomposition result in successive levels of detail?

13. Are modules performing more than one specific function?

Logic

14. Are there any logic errors?

15. Are all unique values tested? All positional values tested? Increment and loop counters properly initialized? Variables and data areas initialized before use?

16. Has the module been inspected for correct begin and end of table processing? Correct processing of queues across interrupts? Correct decision table logic? Correct precision and accuracy of calculations?

17. Are message priorities allocated properly to ensure the correct execution of code?

18. Is the message processing sequence correct?

19. Are there errors in handling data, data buffers, or tables; incorrect field updates; conflicting use of data areas; incomplete initialization or update; inconsistent or invalid data attributes?

20. Are procedure call and return interfaces correctly defined? Call and return parameters defined correctly? Syntax correct?

Performance

21. Are memory and timing budgets reasonable and achievable?

Error Handling and Recovery

22. Is there adequate error condition testing?
23. Are error conditions defined where the probability of an error is high or results of an error would be fatal to the system?
24. Are return codes documented?
25. Are return messages understandable?
26. Does the program allow for successful error recovery from module or process failures? From operating system failure? From interrupts? From hardware failures?

Testability, Extensibility

27. Is the design understandable (i.e., easy to read, to follow logic)? Maintainable (i.e., no obscure logic)? Testable (i.e., can be tested with a reasonable number of tests)?

Coupling and Cohesion

28. Evaluate the design using standard coupling and cohesion criteria, if appropriate.

D.4 Code inspection checklist for C code

1. Is the design implemented completely and correctly?
2. Are there missing or extraneous functions?
3. Is each loop executed the correct number of times?
4. Will each loop terminate?
5. Will the program terminate?
6. Are all possible loop fall-throughs correct?
7. Are all CASE statements evaluated as expected?
8. Is there any unreachable code?
9. Are there any off-by-one iteration errors?
10. Are there any dangling ELSE clauses?
11. Is pointer addressing used correctly?

12. Are priority rules and brackets in arithmetic expression evaluation used as required to achieve desired results?

13. Are boundary conditions considered (null or negative values, adding to an empty list, etc.)?

14. Are pointer parameters used as values and vice versa?

Interfaces

15. Is the number of input parameters equal to the number of arguments?

16. Do parameter and argument attributes match?

17. Do the units of parameters and arguments match?

18. Are any input-only arguments altered?

19. Are global variable definitions consistent across modules?

20. Are any constants passed as arguments?

21. Are any functions called and never returned from?

22. Are returned VOID values used?

23. Are all interfaces correctly used as defined in the SDD?

Data and Storage

24. Are data mode definitions correctly used?

25. Are data and storage areas initialized before use and correct fields accessed and/or updated?

26. Is data scope correctly established and used?

27. If identifiers with identical names exist at different procedure call levels, are they used correctly according to their local and global scope?

28. Is there unnecessary packing or mapping of data?

29. Are all pointers based on correct storage attributes?

30. Is the correct level of indirection used?

31. Are any string limits exceeded?

32. Are all variables explicitly declared?

33. Are all arrays, strings, and pointers initialized correctly?

34. Are all subscripts within bounds?

35. Are there any noninteger subscripts?

Maintainability and Testability

36. Is the code understandable (choice of variable names, use of comments, etc.)?

37. Is there a module header?

38. Is there sufficient and accurate commentary to allow the reader to understand the code?

39. Does the formatting and indenting style add to the readability of the code?

40. Are coding conventions followed?

41. Is tricky or obscure logic used?

42. Is the code structured to allow for easier debugging and testing?

43. Is the code structured so that it can be easily extended for new functions?

44. Are there any unnecessary restrictions due to code structure?

Error Handling

45. Are all probable error conditions handled?

46. Are error messages and return codes used?

47. Are the error messages and return codes meaningful and accurate?

48. Are the default branches in CASE statements handled correctly?

49. Does the code allow for recovery from error conditions?

50. Is range checking done where appropriate to isolate the source of an error?

D.5 A C++ code inspection checklist

Copyright © 1992 by John T. Baldwin. Complete information regarding copyright permission, sources, and distribution appears in Section D.5.20.

D.5.1 Variable declarations

D.5.1.1 Arrays

Is an array dimensioned to a hard-coded constant?

```
int intarray[13];
```

should be

```
int intarray[TOT_MONTHS+1];
```

Is the array dimensioned to the total number of items?

```
char entry[TOTAL_ENTRIES];
```

should be

```
char entry[LAST_ENTRY+1];
```

The first example is extremely error prone and often gives rise to off-by-one errors in the code. The preferred (second) method permits the writer to use the LAST_ENTRY identifier to refer to the last item in the array. Instances that require a buffer of a certain size are rarely rendered invalid by this practice, which results in the buffer being one element bigger than absolutely necessary.

D.5.1.2 Constants

Does the value of the variable never change?

```
int months_in_year = 12;
```

should be

```
const unsigned months_in_year = 12;
```

Are constants declared with the preprocessor #define *mechanism?*

```
#define MAX_FILES 20
```

should be

```
const unsigned MAX_FILES = 20;
```

Is the usage of the constant limited to only a few (or perhaps only one) class? If so, is the constant global?

```
const unsigned MAX_FOOS = 1000;

const unsigned MAX_FOO_BUFFERS = 40;
```

should be

```
class foo {

 public:

  enum { MAX_INSTANCES = 1000; }

 private:

  enum { MAX_FOO_BUFFERS = 40; }

 };
```

If the size of the constant exceeds `int`, another mechanism is available:

```
class bar{

public:

  static const long MAX_INSTS;

 };

const long bar::MAX_INSTS = 70000L;
```

The keyword `static` ensures there is only one instance of the variable for the entire class. Static data items are not permitted to be initialized within the class declaration, so the initialization line must be included in the implementation file for class bar.

Static constant members have one drawback: You cannot use them to declare member data arrays of a certain size. That is because the value is not available to the compiler at the point that the array is declared in the class.

D.5.1.3 Scalar variables

Does a negative value of the variable make no sense? If so, is the variable signed?

```
int age;
```

should be

```
unsigned int age;
```

This is an easy error to make, since the default types are usually signed.

Does the code assume `char` *is either signed or unsigned?*

```
typedef char SmallInt;
```

```
SmallInt mumble = 280;  // WRONG on Borland C++ 3.1 // or
                                    MSC/C++ 7.0!
```

The typedefs should be

```
typedef unsigned char SmallUInt;
```

```
typedef signed char SmallInt;
```

Does the program unnecessarily use float or double?

```
double acct_balance;
```

should be

```
unsigned long acct_balance;
```

In general, the only time floating-point arithmetic is necessary is in scientific or navigational calculations. It is slow and subject to more complex overflow and underflow behavior than integer math is. Monetary calculations can often be handled in counts of cents and formatted properly on output. Thus, `acct_balance` might equal 103446 and print out as $1,034.46.

D.5.1.4 Classes

Does the class have any virtual functions? If so, is the destructor nonvirtual?
Classes having virtual functions should always have a virtual destructor. This is necessary since it is likely that you will hold an object of a class with a pointer of a less derived type. Making the destructor virtual ensures that the right code will be run if you delete the object via the pointer.

Does the class have any of the following:

> Copy-constructor;
>
> Assignment operator;
>
> Destructor.

If so, it generally will need all three. (Exceptions occasionally may be found for some classes having a destructor with neither of the other two.)

D.5.2 Data usage

D.5.2.1 Strings

Can the string ever not be null-terminated?

Is the code attempting to use a `strxxx()` *function on a nonterminated char array, as if it were a string?*

D.5.2.2 Buffers

Are there always size checks when copying into the buffer?

Can the buffer ever be too small to hold its contents?
For example, one program had no size checks when reading data into a buffer because the correct data would always fit. But when the file it read was accidentally overwritten with incorrect data, the program crashed mysteriously.

D.5.2.3 Bitfields

Is a bitfield really required for this application?

Are there possible ordering problems (portability)?

D.5.3 Initialization

D.5.3.1 Local variables

Are local variables initialized before being used?

Are C++ locals created, then assigned later?
This practice has been shown to incur up to 350% overhead, compared to the practice of declaring the variable later in the code, when an initialization variable is known. It is a simple matter of putting a value in once instead of assigning some default value, then later throwing it away and assigning the real value.

D.5.3.2 Missing reinitialization

Can a variable carry an old value forward from one loop iteration to the next?
Suppose the processing of a data element in a sequence causes a variable to be set. For example, a file might be read, and some globals initialized for that file. Can those globals be used for the next file in the sequence without being reinitialized?

D.5.4 Macros

If a macro's formal parameter is evaluated more than once, is the macro ever expanded with a actual parameter having side effects? For example, what happens in the following code?

```
#define max(a,b) ( (a) > (b) ? (a) : (b) )

max(i++, j);
```

If a macro is not completely parenthesized, is it ever invoked in a way that will cause unexpected results?

```
#define max(a, b) (a) > (b) ? (a) : (b) result =
max(i, j) + 3;
```

This expands into:

```
result = (i) > (j) ? (i) : (j)+3;
```

See the example for the first question in this section (D.5.4) for the correct parenthesization.

If the macro's arguments are not parenthesized, will this ever cause unexpected results?

```
#define IsXBitSet(var) (var && bitmask) result =
IsXBitSet( i || j );
```

This expands into:

```
result = (i || j && bitmask); // not what expected!
```

The correct form is:

```
#define IsXBitSet(var) ((var) && (bitmask))
```

D.5.5 Sizing of data

In a function call with arguments for a buffer and its size, is the argument to `sizeof` *different from the buffer argument? For example:*

```
memset(buffer1, 0, sizeof(buffer2)); // danger!
```

This is not always an error, but it is a dangerous practice. Each instance should be verified as (1) necessary and (2) correct and then commented on as such.

Is the argument to `sizeof` *an incorrect type? Common errors include:*

> `sizeof(ptr)` instead of `sizeof(*ptr)`
>
> `sizeof(*array)` instead of `sizeof(array)`
>
> `sizeof(array)` instead of `sizeof(array[0])` (when the user wanted the size of an element)

D.5.6 Dynamic allocation

D.5.6.1 Allocating data

Is too little space being allocated?

Does the code allocate memory and then assume someone else will delete it? This is not always an error, but it should always be prominently documented, along with the reason for implementing it in this manner. Constructors that allocate, paired with destructors that deallocate, are an obvious exception, since a single object has control of its class data.

Is `malloc()`, `calloc()`, *or* `realloc()` *used in lieu of* `new`? C standard library allocation functions should never be used in C++ programs, since C++ provides an allocation operator.

If you find you must mix C allocation with C++ allocation, is `malloc`, `calloc`, *or* `realloc` *invoked for an object that has a constructor? Program behavior is undefined if that is done.*

D.5.6.2 Deallocating data

Are arrays being deleted as if they were scalars?

```
delete myCharArray;
```

should be

```
delete [] myCharArray;
```

Does the deleted storage still have pointers to it? It is recommended that pointers are set to NULL following deletion or to another safe value meaning "uninitialized." This is neither necessary nor recommended within destructors, since the pointer variable itself will cease to exist upon exiting.

Are you deleting already deleted storage? This is not possible if the code conforms to the answer to the preceding question. The draft C++ standard specifies that it is always safe to delete a NULL pointer, so it is not necessary to check for that value.

If C standard library allocators are used in a C++ program (not recommended), is `delete` *invoked on a pointer obtained via* `malloc`, `calloc`, *or* `realloc`?

Is `free` *invoked on a pointer obtained via* `new`? Both these practices are dangerous. Program behavior is undefined if you do them, and such usage is specifically deprecated by the ANSI draft C++ standard.

D.5.7 Pointers

When dereferenced, can the pointer ever be NULL?

When copying the value of a pointer, should it instead allocate a copy of what the first pointer points to?

D.5.8 Casting

Is NULL cast to the correct type when passed as a function argument?

Does the code rely on an implicit type conversion?
C++ is somewhat charitable when arguments are passed to functions: If no function is found that exactly matches the types of the arguments supplied, it attempts to apply certain type conversion rules to find a match. While this saves unnecessary casting, if more than one function fits the conversion rules, it will result in a compilation error. Worse, it can cause additions to the type system (either from adding a related class or from adding an overloaded function) to cause previously working code to break!

See Section D.5.17 for an example.

D.5.9 Computation

When the value of an assignment or computation is tested, is the parenthesization incorrect?

```
if ( a = function() == 0 )
```

should be

```
if ( (a = function()) == 0 )
```

Can any synchronized values not get updated?
Sometimes, a group of variables must be modified as a group to complete a single conceptual "transaction." If that does not occur all in one place, is it guaranteed that all variables get updated if a single value changes? Do all updates occur before any of the values are tested or used?

D.5.10 Conditionals

Are exact equality tests used on floating point numbers?

```
if ( someVar == 0.1 )
```

might never be evaluated as true. The constant 0.1 is not exactly representable by any finite binary mantissa and exponent; thus, the compiler must round it to some other number. Calculations involving `someVar` may never result in it taking on that value.

The solution is to use >,> =,<, or <= depending on which direction you want the variable bound.

Are unsigned values tested greater than or equal to zero?

```
if ( myUnsignedVar = 0 )
```

will always evaluate true.

Are signed variables tested for equality to zero or another constant?

```
if ( mySignedVar )  // not always good
```

```
if ( mySignedVar = 0 )  // better!
```

```
if ( mySignedVar 0 )  // opposite case
```

If the variable is updated by any means other than ++ or − −, it may miss the value of the test constant entirely. That can cause subtle and frightening bugs when code executes under conditions that were not planned for.

If the test is an error check, could the error condition actually be legitimate in some cases?

D.5.11 Flow control

D.5.11.1 Control variables

Is the lower limit an exclusive limit?

Is the upper limit an inclusive limit?
By always using inclusive lower limits and exclusive upper limits, a whole class of off-by-one errors is eliminated. Furthermore, the following assumptions always apply:

- The size of the interval equals the difference of the two limits.
- The limits are equal if the interval is empty.

- The upper limit is never less than the lower limit.
- For example, instead of saying x>=23 and x<=42, use x>=23 and x<43.

D.5.11.2 Branching

In a switch statement, is any case not terminated with a break statement?
When several cases are followed by the same block of code, they may be stacked and the code terminated with a single break.

Cases may also be exited via return.

All other circumstances requiring "drop-through" cases should be clearly documented in a strategic comment before the switch. This should be used only when it makes the code simpler and clearer.

Does the switch statement lack a default branch?
There should always be a default branch to handle unexpected cases, even when it appears that the code can never get there.

Does a loop set a boolean flag to effect an exit?
Consider using break instead. It is likely to simplify the code.

Does the loop contain a continue?
If the continue occurs in the body of an if conditional, consider replacing it with an else clause if it will simplify the code.

D.5.12 Assignment

D.5.12.1 Assignment operators

Does a += b mean something different than a = a + b?
The programmer should never change the semantics of relationships between operators. For the example here, the two statements are semantically identical for intrinsic types (even though the code generated might be different), so for a user-defined class, they should be semantically identical, too. They may, in fact, be implemented differently (+= should be more efficient).

Is the argument for a copy constructor or assignment operator non const?

Does the assignment operator fail to test for self-assignment?
The code for operator=() should always start out with:

```
if (this == &right_hand_arg )
```

```
return *this;
```

Does the assignment operator return anything other than a const *reference to this?*
Failure to return a reference to this prevents the user from writing (legal C++):

```
a = b = c;
```

Failure to make the return reference const allows the user to write (illegal C++):

```
(a = b) = c;
```

D.5.12.2 Use of assignment

Can this assignment be replaced with an initialization?
See the second question in Section D.5.3.1.

Is there a mismatch between the units of the expression and those of the variable?
For example, you might be calculating the number of bytes for an array when the number of elements was requested. If the elements are big (say, a long or a struct!), you would be using way too much memory.

D.5.13 Argument passing

Are nonintrinsic-type arguments passed by value?

```
Foo& do_something( Foo anotherFoo, Bar someThing );
```

should be

```
Foo& do_something( const Foo& anotherFoo, const
Bar& someThing );
```

While it is cheaper to pass an int, a long, and such by value, passing objects that way incurs significant expense due to the construction of temporary objects. The problem becomes more severe when inheritance is involved. Simulate pass-by-value by passing const references.

D.5.14 Return values

Is the return value of a function call being stored in a type that is too narrow?
See Section D.5.18.

Does a public member function return a non `const` *reference or pointer to member data?*

Does a public member function return a non `const` *reference or pointer to data outside the object?*
This is permissible, provided the data were intended to be shared, and that fact is documented in the source code.

Does an operator return a reference when it should return an object?

Are objects returned by value instead of `const` *references?*
See the question in Section D.5.13.

D.5.15 Function calls

D.5.15.1 `Varargs` Functions (`printf` and Other Functions With Ellipses)

Is the FILE argument of `fprintf` *missing? (This happens all the time.)*

Are there extra arguments?

Do the argument types explicitly match the conversion specifications in the format string? (`printf` *and friends.)*
Type checking cannot occur for functions with variable length argument lists. For example, a user was surprised to see nonsensical values when the following code was executed:

```
printf(" %d %ld \n", a_long_int, another_long_int);
```

On that particular system, `int` s and `long` s were different sizes (2 and 4 bytes, respectively). `printf()` is responsible for manually accessing the stack; thus, it saw "`%d`" and grabbed 2 bytes (an `int`).

It then saw "`%ld`" and grabbed 4 bytes (a long). The two values printed were the MSW of `a_long_int`, and the combination of `a_long_int`'s LSW and `another_long_int`'s MSW.

The solution is to ensure that types explicitly match. If necessary, arguments may be cast to smaller sizes (`long` to `int`) if the author knows for certain that the smaller type can hold all possible values of the variable.

D.5.15.2 General functions

Is this function call correct? That is, should it be a different function with a similar name (e.g., `strchr` *instead of* `strrchr`*)?*

Can this function violate the preconditions of a called function?

D.5.16 Files

Can a temporary file name not be unique? (Surprisingly enough, this is a common design bug.)

Is a file pointer reused without closing the previous file?

```
fp = fopen(...);

fp = fopen(...);
```

Is a file not closed in case of an error return?

D.5.17 Errors due to implicit type conversions

Code that relies on implicit type conversions may become broken when new classes or functions are added. For example:

```
class String {

public:

String( char *arg ); // copy constructor operator const char*
() const;

...

};

void foo( const String& aString );

void bar( const char *anArray );
```

Now, we added the following class

```
class Word {

public:

Word( char *arg );  // copy constructor

. . .

};
```

need another foo that works with "Words"

```
void foo( const Word& aWord );

int gorp()

{

foo("hello");  // This used to work!  Now it breaks!  What gives?

String baz = "quux";

bar(baz);  // but this still works.

}
```

The code worked before class Word and the second foo() were added. Even though there was no foo() accepting an argument of type const char * (i.e., a constant string like "hello"), there is a foo() that takes a constant String argument by reference. And (un)fortunately, there is also a way to convert a Strings to a char * and vice versa. So the compiler performed the implicit conversion.

Now, with the addition of class Word and another foo() that works with it, there is a problem. The line that calls foo("hello") matches both:

```
void foo( const String& );

void foo( const Word& );
```

Since the mechanisms of the failure may be distributed among two or more header files in addition to the implementation file, along with a lot of other code, it may be difficult to find the real problem.

The easiest solution is to recognize while coding or inspecting that a function call results in implicit type conversion and either (1) overload the function to provide an explicitly typed variant or (2) explicitly cast the argument.

Option 1 is preferred over option 2, because option 2 defeats automatic type checking. Option 1 can still be implemented efficiently, simply by writing the new function as a forwarding function and making it inline.

D.5.18 Errors due to loss of "precision" in return values

Functions that can return EOF should not have their return values stored in a `char` variable. For example:

```
int getchar(void);

char chr;

while ( (chr = getchar()) != EOF ) { ... };
```

should be:

```
int tmpchar;

while ( (tmpchar = getchar()) != EOF ) {

   chr = (char) tmpchar;  // or use casted tmpchar throughout

};
```

The practice in the first example is unsafe because functions like `getchar()` may return 257 different values: valid characters with indexes 0–255, plus EOF (−1). If `sizeof(int)` > `sizeof(char)`, then information will be lost when the high-order byte(s) are scraped off prior to the test for EOF. This can cause the test to fail. Worse yet, depending on whether `char` is signed or unsigned by default on the particular compiler and machine being used, sign extension can wreak havoc and cause some of these loops never to terminate.

D.5.19 Loop checklist

The following loops are indexed correctly and are handy for comparisons during inspections. If the actual code does not look like one of these, chances are that something is wrong or, at least, could be clearer.

Acceptable forms of `for` loops that avoid off-by-one errors are:

```
for ( i = 0; i max_index; ++i )

for ( i = 0; i sizeof(array); ++i )

for ( i = max_index; i>= 0; --i )

for ( i = max_index; i ; --i )
```

D.5.20 Copyright notices

Some of the questions applicable to conventional C contained herein were modified or taken from *A Question Catalog for Code Inspections,* Copyright 1992 by Brian Marick. Portions of his document were Copyright 1991 by Motorola, Inc., which graciously granted him rights to those portions.

In conformance with his copyright notice, the following contact information is provided below:

Brian Marick Testing Foundations 809 Balboa, Champaign, IL 61820

marick@cs.uiuc.edu, marick@testing.com

"You may copy or modify this document for personal use, provided you retain the original copyright notice and contact information."

Some questions and comment material were modified from *Programming in C++, Rules and Recommendations,* Copyright 1990–1992 by Ellemtel Telecommunication Systems Laboratories.

In conformance with their copyright notice:

"Permission is granted to any individual or institution to use, copy, modify, and distribute this document, provided that this complete copyright and permission notice is maintained intact in all copies."

Finally, all modifications and remaining original material are:

Copyright 1992 by John T. Baldwin. All Rights Reserved.

John T. Baldwin 1511 Omie Way Lawrenceville, GA 30243

Permission is granted to any institution or individual to copy, modify, distribute, and use this document, provided that the complete copyright, permission, and contact information applicable to all copyright holders specified herein remains intact in all copies of this document.

D.6 Test procedure inspection checklist

1. Does each test have a header that identifies the author, revision date, test objectives, required configuration, and initial setup?

2. Is each test traceable to a specific requirement defined in the SDD or the SRS?

3. Does the test procedure define the exact sequence of steps required to execute the test?

4. For each test, are the expected results clearly defined?

5. Are the expected results consistent with the SRS and the SDD?

6. Are the test objectives achievable?

Appendix E

Attributes of good requirements specifications

Good requirements specifications have the following attributes:

- *Unambiguous.* The SRS is unambiguous if and only if every requirement has only one interpretation.

- *Complete.* The SRS is complete if it contains all significant requirements that relate to functionality, performance, timing, design constraints, attributes, external interfaces, and so on. A complete SRS also contains a definition of the response of the software to all known classes of inputs in all known situations

- *Verifiable.* The SRS is verifiable if and only if every requirement is verifiable. A requirement is verifiable if and only if there is some finite, cost-effective process by which a human being or a machine can verify that the software correctly implements the stated requirements.

- *Consistent.* The SRS is consistent if and only if individual requirements do not conflict.
- *Modifiable.* The SRS is modifiable if its structure and style are such that unanticipated changes can be made easily, completely, and consistently.
- *Traceable.* The SRS is traceable if each requirement is clearly traceable to a statement contained in the preceding document and if the SRS facilitates the referencing of requirements to subsequent documents (such as the SDD).
- *Usable.* The SRS must provide suffcient information to be usable during the maintenance phase of the product lifecycle since it is likely that different people will be involved with product maintenance activities.

Appendix F

Sample criteria for selecting modules for code inspection

You can use the following sample criteria to help select modules for code inspection. Revise this list based on criteria important to your project or organization.

- *Criticality*. The module performs a function or functions critical to the correct operation of the end product.

- *Complexity*. The module is determined to be more complex than other modules based on an evaluation by a complexity metric, such as the McCabe cyclomatic complexity or Halstead software science metric.

- *Past history*. In the past, a relatively high number of bugs have been found in modules that perform similar functions.

- *Experience level of software engineer*. The software engineer who wrote the code is relatively inexperienced.

Appendix G

Sample software development process based on the waterfall model

For each phase of the process, the following information is included:

- Purpose;
- Activities;
- Deliverables;
- Tools;
- Exit Criteria;
- Metrics.

Note: Software V&V-related items are indicated with an asterisk.

G.1 Requirements analysis phase

Purpose

- Develop product concept;
- Allocate requirements to hardware and software (if appropriate).

Activities

- Conduct market research;
- Write business plan;
- Write product concept document;
- Create RTM.*

Deliverables

- Product concept document;
- Business plan.

Tools
- Requirements tracing tool;
- Market research tools (e.g., conjoint analysis).

Exit Criteria

- Concept specification reviewed and approved;
- Business plan reviewed and approved;
- RTM created.

Metrics

- Person-hours expended to date;
- Number of testable requirements identified;
- Number of untestable requirements identified.

G.2 Requirements definition phase

Purpose

- Define requirements to be implemented by software.

Activities

- Refine requirements contained in concept specification;
- Define user interface metaphors (if appropriate);
- Write SRS;
- Conduct a requirements inspection on the SRS*;
- Update the RTM.*

Deliverables

- SRS;
- User interface metaphors (if appropriate; can be expressed in the form of a style guide);
- Software development plan;
- Software V&V plan.*

Tools

- Performance analysis tools;
- Structured analysis and information modeling tools;
- Requirements tracing tool.

Exit Criteria

- SRS, software development plan, and software V&V plan approved;
- Requirements inspection held on SRS;
- User interface style guide prepared (if appropriate).

Metrics

- Completeness of RTM*;
- Number and type of errors and defects found during requirements inspection of SRS.*

G.3 Design phase

Purpose

- Develop a clear, concise, and consistent design;
- Establish a controlled environment for the coding phase.

Activities

- Develop overall software architecture;
- Develop high-level software design;
- Develop detailed software design;
- Conduct design inspections*;
- Develop software architecture, high-level software design and detailed software design specifications;
- Begin development of software validation test procedures based on SRS*;
- Develop software reliability growth plan*;
- Evaluate and select SCM and SPR tracking tools*;
- Evaluate and select automated software validation testing tools*;
- Update RTM.*

Deliverables

- Software architecture, high-level design specification(s), detailed design specifications;
- Software validation test procedures*;
- SCM plan*;
- Software validation test plan*;
- Software reliability growth plan*;
- Alpha and beta test plans (if appropriate).*

Tools

- Structured design and information modeling tools;
- Detailed design tools (data flow diagrams, state transition matrices, etc.);
- Performance analysis tools;

- Configuration management tools;
- Automated software validation testing tools;
- Software problem report tracking tool;
- Requirements tracing tools.

Exit Criteria

- Software architecture reviewed and approved;
- Software design specifications approved;
- Design inspections held*;
- SCM plan reviewed and approved*;
- SCM tools selected and in place*;
- Software validation test plan and alpha and beta test plans reviewed and approved.*

Metrics

- Completeness of RTM*;
- Number and type of errors and defects found during design inspections.*

G.4 Coding phase

Purpose

- Write code that implements the requirements contained in the SRS as expressed by the overall architecture and further defined by the design specifications.

Activities

- Develop code;
- Conduct code inspections on selected modules*;
- Perform unit and integration testing;
- Implement SCM procedures*;
- Implement software problem reporting procedures*;
- Implement software reliability growth tracking procedures*;

- Apply selected software quality metrics to modules*;
- Complete development of software validation test procedures based on SRS*;
- Conduct software validation test procedure inspections*;
- Develop software release procedures*;
- Update product documentation (concept specification, SRS, and SDDs);
- Conduct software validation readiness review*;
- Update RTM.*

Deliverables

- Source code;
- Software validation test procedures*;
- Software reliability growth procedures*;
- Software release procedure*;
- Software problem reports.*

Tools

- Coding tools (compilers, debuggers, lint, etc.);
- Quality metric tools (e.g., code complexity);
- SCM tools;
- Software problem report tracking tools;
- Automated software validation test tools;
- Software reliability growth tracking tools;
- Requirement tracing tools.

Exit Criteria

- Coding completed;
- All source code under configuration management control;
- Software problem report tracking in place*;
- Software reliability growth tracking in place*;
- Software validation readiness review held*;

- Software validation test procedures approved*;
- Test procedure inspections held*;
- All software validation test procedures executed at least once.*

Metrics

- Number and type or errors and defects found during code inspections*;
- Number and type of errors and defects found during test procedure inspections*;
- Complexity and quality metrics for each module*;
- Size of each module (lines of source code)*;
- Size of final executable (number of bytes)*;
- Completeness of RTM.*

G.5 Testing phase

Purpose

- To determine if the software meets requirements defined in the SRS.

Activities

- Execute software validation test procedures*;
- Track and resolve problems identified as a result of executing tests*;
- Perform regression testing as required*;
- Fix bugs and release new versions for validation testing.

Deliverables

- Software validation test report*;
- Final version of software for release.

Tools

- Automated software validation testing tools;
- Software problem report tracking tool;
- SCM tools;

- Coding and debugging tools;
- Requirements traceability tools.

Exit Criteria

- Software validation testing completion criteria met*;
- Software validation test report reviewed and approved.*

Metrics

- Find/fix time for bugs*;
- Test coverage metrics*;
- Software reliability growth metrics.*

G.6 Maintenance phase

Purpose

- Provide ongoing product support after release.

Activities

- Fix known defects;
- Change software to correct deficiencies in other parts of the product;
- Add new features or enhance existing features;
- Extensive testing based on changes made.*
- Regression testing*;
- Update product documentation (SRS, SDDs, test procedures, etc.).

Deliverables

- New releases of software;
- Updated product documentation.

Tools

- Same tools used in earlier phases.

Exit Criteria

- Decision made to discontinue supporting the product.

Metrics

- Number and type of bugs reported by customers;
- Number and type of new features requested by customers;
- Find/fix time for bugs.

Appendix H

Document outlines

This appendix includes outlines for the following documents:

- Product concept document;
- Software requirements specification (SRS);
- Software design description (SDD);
- Software development plan (SDP);
- Software quality assurance plan (SQAP);
- Software validation test plan;
- Software validation test procedure;
- Software validation test report;
- Software validation test script;
- Software configuration management plan;
- Software release procedure.

The following information is included for each document:

- Purpose and target audience;
- Outline.

H.1 Product concept document

H.1.1 Purpose and target audience

The purpose of the product concept document is to define overall product goals as well as high-level requirements the product must meet. The target audience for this document includes the project team, marketing, and management.

H.1.2 Outline

H.1.2.1 Overview

- Product features and benefits;
- Market requirements;
- Target markets;
- Competitive analysis;
- Desired launch window.

H.1.2.2 Product goals

- Usability goals;
- Reliability goals;
- Upgradability goals;
- Serviceability goals;
- Maintainability goals.

H.1.2.3 Product functional requirements

- Functional requirements;
- Performance requirements;
- Timing requirements.

H.1.2.4 Financial requirements

- Cost requirements;
- Projected selling price.

H.2 Software requirements specification (SRS)

H.2.1 Purpose and target audience

The purpose of this document is to define the requirements that have been allocated to software. By far, this document is the most important document written for a software development effort. The SRS forms the basis for software design, software validation, development of technical manuals, development of training materials, etc. The target audience for this document includes software engineering, SQA, marketing, and technical publications.

H.2.2 Outline

Reference: IEEE-STD-830-1984.

H.2.2.1 Product overview

Product Perspective
This section places the SRS into perspective with regard to other products and/or projects. Dependencies between this product and other products and/or projects should be clearly stated. Include block diagrams showing major components, external interfaces, and interconnections where appropriate.

Product Functions
Provide a brief summary of the product functions and categorize these functions into related groups for ease of understanding. A key element to include in this section is the feature release plan. This plan identifies specific features that will be included in a sequence of planned releases.

H.2.2.2 General constraints

This section describes items that limit the available options for software design. For example:

- Hardware limitations;
- Interface requirements to other systems and/or products;
- Communication protocols that must be supported;

- Criticality of operations;
- Conformance to accepted standards.

H.2.2.3 Assumptions and dependencies

Identify specific assumptions and dependencies that affect requirements.

H.2.2.4 User interface

Describe in detail the user interface for the product. This should include screen layouts for all expected screens and all anticipated user interaction and input devices. If necessary, a user interface style guide may need to be developed for a new or radically different user interface.

H.2.2.5 Specific requirements

This section contains the functional requirements that the software must implement. There are many ways to organize the information in this section. The referenced IEEE standard includes three options. Use the method most appropriate for the intended users of the document.

H.2.2.6 Introduction

Inputs
Describe sources of inputs, quantities, ranges and limits, accuracy and tolerance, timing issues, units, etc.

Processing
Describe all operations performed on the input data and intermediate parameters to obtain the desired output. Include equations, algorithms, logical operations, validity checks on input data, sequences of operations, timing issues, etc. Also, address responses to abnormal situations, such as buffer overflow, communications failures, etc. Provide requirements for degraded operation, if required.

Outputs
Describe in detail destination/use of outputs, quantities, units, timing issues, range of valid outputs, error handling, etc.

H.2.2.7 Requirements

- Performance requirements;
- Diagnostics requirements;
- Security requirements;

- Maintainability requirements;
- Configurability requirements;
- Upgradability requirements
- Testability requirements;
- Installability requirements.

H.2.2.8 Appendixes

- Communications protocols;
- Supporting information for algorithms;
- Index of requirements.

H.3 Software design description (SDD)

H.3.1 Purpose and target audience

The purpose of the SDD is to describe the design of the software. The target audience for this document includes software engineering and SQA.

H.3.2 Outline

Reference: IEEE Std 1016-1987.

The following is one of many ways to organize and format the information required for the SDD. Refer to the IEEE standard for alternatives more suited to your particular environment.

H.3.2.1 Decomposition description

The decomposition description records the division of the software into design entities. It describes the way the software has been structured. It also defines the purpose, function, subordinates, and type of each software design entity.

H.3.2.2 Dependency description

The dependency description specifies the relationships among entities. It identifies the dependent entities, describes their coupling, and identifies the required resources.

H.3.2.3 Interface description

The interface description provides everything designers, programmers, and testers need to know to correctly use the functions provided by an entity. This description includes details of the internal and external interfaces not included in the software requirements document.

H.3.2.4 Detailed design

This section contains the detailed design for each of the entities identified above. These details include attribute descriptions for identification, processing, and data.

H.4 Software development plan (SDP)

H.4.1 Purpose and target audience

The purpose of the SDP is to document a common understanding of the software development activities that will occur during a development project. The plan describes the role of the software development team within the context of the development project, the process that will be used to develop the software, the inputs that must be provided to develop the software, and what will be delivered as a result of following the SDP. The SDP also establishes the development schedule and the tools and staffing that will be required. The reason to document this understanding is to eliminate ambiguity and assumptions, provide a means of measuring progress and success, and a method for continuous improvement.

The SDP is the primary document that will be used in conducting all audits of the software development process for the project. It should reference the company's software development process wherever possible. If the project will deviate from the software development process, the nature of the deviation must be described and justified in the plan. For large or complex projects, the individual sections of the SDP can be handled as separate documents. These separate documents should then be referenced in the SDP.

The target audience for the SDP includes the project team, management, software engineering, and SQA.

H.4.2 Outline

H.4.2.1 Introduction

H.4.2.2 Project definition

Goals
This section describes the overall goals of the software. These goals include not only product specific goals but also any other goals, such as commonality, future projects, staff development, etc.

Deliverables
This section defines all the deliverables from the software team.

H.4.2.3 Project context

Project teams
This section of the SDP describes all other teams working on the same project that directly influence the SDP. Entities to be considered include:

- Marketing;
- Manufacturing;
- SQA;
- Technical publications;
- Training;
- Technical support.

Team Interfaces
This section of the SDP defines the interfaces between the software development team and other project teams detailed above.

H.4.2.4 Development strategy

Process model
Describe the software development life cycle to be used. This description includes dependencies, timing of reviews, baselines, deliverables, and milestones. If there are any timing requirements for input documentation, they should also be described here. This section should describe any special mechanisms that will be used to control the software development process.

Target environment

This section describes any assumptions made regarding the target environment for software development. Examples of assumptions to highlight includes the number and the type of processors being used, the user interface devices available, memory, and disk space.

Build vs. buy

This section defines the criteria that will be used for determining what portions of the software system will be purchased, subcontracted, or developed in house.

Team organization

This section describes the organization of the software development team including the structure of the team, responsibilities of each part of the team, and formal reporting methods and frequency.

Constraints

Describe any constraints on the software development that are not explicitly described elsewhere. These may include budgetary, timing, staffing, and operational constraints.

Metrics

Describe the measurements that will be made to ensure adherence to this plan, for monitoring progress, and for establishing the quality of the deliverables.

H.4.2.5 Methodologies

This section describes the methods, policies, procedures, and techniques to be used in the creation, modification, review, testing, measurement, and maintenance of the deliverables.

H.4.2.6 Standards

This section of the SDP describes the technical standards to be applied to any and all deliverables from the development effort and how adherence to the standards will be measured, for example, coding standards, naming conventions, notations, and requirements format.

H.4.2.7 Resource requirements

Staffing plan

This section of the SDP describes the staffing plan for the software development:

- Skill set needed;

- Whether skills will be developed internally or hired;
- Number of people needed;
- Ramp-up and ramp-down plans.

Tools

This section describes the tools that will be used for the development of the software. Examples of the types of tools to be addressed include:

- Development computers;
- Word processors;
- Compilers;
- CASE tools;
- Revision control systems;
- Debuggers;
- Prototype target hardware.

Support functions

This section describes any and all support functions, either required or provided by the software development team, not explicitly described elsewhere. Examples might include external integration testing support, external requirements traceability support, and external revision control.

H.4.2.8 Schedules

Provide an estimated schedule of the software development effort and describe the major activities called out in the process model and the staffing levels required. For large projects, the schedule should be called out as a separate document, because it is likely to undergo a large number of changes during the course of the project.

H.4.2.9 Risks and risk management

This section describes the primary risk factors associated with the successful implementation of the plan and how those risk factors will be managed. Where appropriate, contingency plans should also be included. Examples of risk factors to consider include:

- New technology;
- Target environment limitations;
- Human resources;

- Budget;
- Schedules.

H.4.2.10 Appendixes

- References;
- Documents;
- Standards;
- Glossary and acronyms.

H.5 Software quality assurance plan (SQAP)

H.5.1 Purpose and target audience

The purpose of the SQAP is to define the processes and procedures used to ensure that software developed for a particular product is of the highest possible quality and meets all its requirements.

The SQAP defines the SQA tasks and when they are performed in relation to activities defined in the SDP. This plan also identifies the additional documents that need to be written. For example, the SQAP may call for separate plans to address software verification, software validation, and configuration management activities. Alternatively, these areas can be addressed within the structure of the SQAP.

The target audience for this document includes SQA and software engineering.

H.5.2 Outline

Reference: IEEE-STD-730.1-1989

H.5.2.1 Management

Organization
Describe the organizational structure that influences and controls the quality of the software.

Tasks
Describe the portion of the software lifecycle model covered by this plan, the tasks to be performed, with emphasis on SQA activities, and the relationship between those tasks and major project milestones.

Responsibilities
Identify the specific organizational elements responsible for each task.

H.5.2.2 Documentation

This section identifies the documents governing the development, verification, validation, use, and maintenance of the software and identifies how those documents are checked for adequacy. This includes identification of the specific review or audit held to review each document.

H.5.2.3 Standards, practices, conventions, and metrics

Identify the standards, practices, conventions, and metrics to be used and state how compliance with these items is to be monitored and assured.

H.5.2.4 Reviews and audits

This section defines the technical and managerial reviews and audits to be conducted, states how the reviews and audits are to be performed, and states what further actions are required and how they are to be implemented and verified.

H.5.2.5 Testing

This section states requirements for testing other than software validation testing. Specifically, unit test, integration test, and performance test requirements should be identified. Software validation testing is described in the software validation test plan.

H.5.2.6 Problem reporting and corrective action

Describe methods and procedures for problem reporting and corrective action as well as the organizational elements responsible for their implementation.

H.5.2.7 Tools, techniques, and methodologies

Identify special tools, techniques, and methodologies required.

H.5.2.8 Code control

Define the methods and facilities used to maintain, store, secure, and document controlled versions of the identified software during all phases of the software lifecycle. For larger projects, this may be implemented by writing an SCM plan.

H.5.2.9 Media control

Define the methods and facilities used to identify the media for each software product and to protect the physical media from unauthorized access, inadvertent damage, or degradation during all phases of the software lifecycle.

H.5.2.10 Supplier control

This section defines the process and procedures for assuring that software provided by suppliers meets established requirements.

H.5.2.11 Records collection, maintenance, and retention

This section defines the SQA documentation to be retained and the methods used to assemble, safeguard, and maintain that documentation and designates the retention period.

H.5.2.13 Training

This section identifies the training required to meet the needs of the SQAP.

H.5.2.14 Risk management

This section defines the methods and procedures used to identify, assess, monitor, and control areas of risk.

H.6 Software validation test plan

H.6.1 Purpose and Target Audience

The software validation test plan describes the process used to perform software validation testing. This plan identifies the resources required for software validation based on estimating the number of tests required. This estimate is derived from the system requirements document and/or the software functional requirements document. This plan also defines the completion criteria used to determine when the software validation task is completed.

The SQAP defines the requirements that must be met in terms of software validation documentation. This test plan is intended to be consistent with the requirements of the SQAP.

The target audience for this document includes the project team and software engineering.

H.6.2 Outline

Reference: IEEE-Std 1012-1986.

H.6.2.1 Software validation overview

Organization

Describe the organization of the validation effort and the relationship of this organization to other organizations such as, development, project management, quality assurance, configuration management, and document control.

Tasks

Identify the specific tasks to be performed as part of software validation. Typically, such tasks would include:

- Test estimation;
- Test script development;
- Test script execution;
- Test script reviews;
- Problem reporting;
- Problem resolution;
- Performing a baseline change assessment;
- Configuration management;
- Regression testing;
- Code inspections;
- Test report;
- Release process.

Responsibilities

Identify the organization responsible for each validation task.

H.6.2.2 Documentation

Identify the documents produced as part of the software validation task. As a minimum, these documents would include:

- Software validation test procedure;
- Software validation test report;
- Software problem reports.

H.6.2.3 Reviews and audits

Identify the reviews and audits held as part of the software validation task. As a minimum, these reviews and audits would include:

- Software validation readiness review (refer to the SQAP);
- Test script reviews;
- Code inspections for modules changed as a result of problem reports.

H.6.2.4 Problem reporting and corrective action

Describe the methods and procedures for problem reporting and corrective action as well as the organizational elements responsible for their implementation. Refer to SQAP, if appropriate.

H.6.2.5 Tools, techniques, and methodologies

Identify special tools, techniques, and methodologies required to support validation functions. Refer to SQAP, if appropriate.

H.6.2.6 Configuration control

Define the methods and facilities used to maintain, store, secure, and document controlled versions of the identified software during all phases of the software lifecycle. Refer to the SQAP, if appropriate. This may be implemented in conjunction with an SCM plan.

H.6.2.7 Test estimates and schedules

Include estimates of the number of software validation test scripts required based on requirements defined in the software requirements document. Based on the estimated number of tests, and using past performance of test development time, project the schedule for test development and test execution.

H.6.2.8 Resource requirements

Identify the resource requirements (equipment, people, computers, bench space, etc.) required to perform software validation testing.

H.6.2.9 Completion criteria

Define the criteria that will be used to determine when software validation is completed. For example, the following criteria should be considered:

- All of the test scripts have been executed.
- All SPRs have been satisfactorily resolved.

- All changes made as a result of SPRs have been tested.
- The projected software reliability growth meets the reliability goal for software.
- The test coverage metric indicates that at least 95% of the code has been executed. A statement identifying the 5% of the code has not been executed and why is included in the software validation test report.

H.7 Software validation test procedure

H.7.1 Purpose and target audience

The test procedure document contains the detailed test scripts that will be run as part of software validation. The target audience for this document includes software engineering and manufacturing.

H.7.2 Outline

- Organization and responsibilities;
- Overview of test scripts;
- Appendix;
- Detailed test scripts (as shown in Section H.8).

H.8 Software validation test script

H.8.1 Purpose and target audience

The test scripts document the specifics of the testing that is performed. This document is intended for software validation testing staff.

Test Script Header
Test Identifier: _____
Test Category: _____
Developed by: _____
Latest Rev: _____

Test Log:

Engineer	Date	Version	SPRs found	SPRs Verified

Test Objectives:
1.
2.
3.

Hardware:
1.
2.
3.

Initial Setup:
1.
2.
3.

Test Script
Initial Test Setup

Detailed Steps
1. Perform step 1   [ ]
   Expected results for step 1

2. Perform step 2   [ ]
   Expected results for step 2

3. Perform step 3   [ ]
   Expected results for step 3
   etc...

Notes and Observations:

H.9 Software validation test report

H.9.1 Purpose and target audience

The purpose of this report is to document the results of software validation testing. The target audience for this document includes software engineering and manufacturing.

H.9.2 Outline

- Organization and responsibilities;
- Summary of results;
- Summary by software version;
- Metrics;
- Conclusions and recommendations;
- Appendixes;
- Completed test scripts;
- Software problem reports.

H.10 Software configuration management plan

H.10.1 Purpose and target audience

The purpose of this plan is to define the methods to be used to identify software products, control and implement changes, and record and report change implementation status. An SCM plan normally would be written for complex projects that involve a large number of software engineers. The target audience for this document includes software engineering and SQA.

H.10.2 Outline

Reference: IEEE-STD-828-1983.

H.10.2.1 Management

Organization
Describe the organizational structure that influences the configuration management of the software during development.

Responsibilities

This section describes the organization element responsible for each configuration management task.

Interface control

This section defines the methods used to perform the following activities:

- Identify interface specifications and control documents;
- Process changes to released documents;
- Provide follow-up on action items;
- Maintain status of interface specifications and control documents;
- Control the interface between the software and the hardware on which it is running.

H.10.2.2 Implementation

This section establishes the major milestones for the implementation of the SCM plan.

Applicable policies, directives, and procedures

This section identifies all policies and procedures related to configuration management that are to be implemented as part of this plan.

H.10.2.3 Activities

Configuration identification

This section defines the procedures for identifying software baselines.

Configuration control

This section defines the procedures for controlling changes to software baselines.

Configuration status accounting

This section defines the procedures for accounting for changes to software baselines.

Audits and reviews

This section defines the role of configuration management in audits and reviews.

H.10.2.4 Tools, techniques, and methodologies

Describe the specific tools, techniques, and methodologies used to perform the configuration management functions.

Supplier control
Describe the procedure for ensuring that vendor-supplied software meets the requirements of this plan.

Records collection and retention
This section defines the configuration management documentation to be retained and the methods used to assemble, safeguard, and maintain this documentation and designates the retention period.

H.11 Software release procedure

H.11.1 Purpose and target audience

The purpose of this procedure is to define the process used to release software from product development to manufacturing. The target audience for this document includes software engineering and manufacturing.

H.11.2 Outline

H.11.2.1 Organization and responsibilities

H.11.2.2 Overview of software release process

H.11.2.3 System requirements

Identify the hardware and software required to create new baselines of software.

H.11.2.4 Configuration management requirements

Identify the configuration management requirements used to establish and control changes to each new baseline of software. Refer to the SCM plan if appropriate.

H.11.2.5 Procedure for creating new baselines

Describe the procedure for creating new baselines.

H.11.2.6 Software validation requirements

Describe the software validation testing performed on each baseline. Refer to the software validation test procedure and the software validation test report.

H.11.2.7 Manufacturing validation requirements

Describe the validation activities performed by manufacturing on each baseline received from product development. Refer to the appropriate manufacturing procedures.

H.11.2.8 Software release sign-off requirements

Define the software release sign-off process. A form should be used with the appropriate signatures to attest to the fact that the requirements of this software release procedure have been followed.

H.11.2.9 Appendix

Include the software release sign-off form.

Appendix   I

Test cases for triangle program

This appendix describes test cases for testing the triangle program described in Chapter 9. The information is from Myers [1].

Test Case Objective	Notes
1. Valid scalene triangle	Test cases such as 1, 2, 3 and 2, 5, 10 do not warrant a 'yes' answer because there does not exist a triangle havcing such sides.
2. Valid equilateral triangle	
3. Valid isosceles triangle	Note that a test case specifying 2, 2, 4 would not be counted.
4. Test cases that represent valid isosceles triangles such that you have covered all three permutations of two equal sides	For example 3, 3, 4,; 3 4, 3; and 4, 3, 3.
5. One side has a value of zero	
6. One side has a negative value	

Test Case Objective	Notes
7. Three integers greater than zero such that the sum of two of the numbers is equal to the third	If the program said that 1, 2, 3 represents a scalene triangle, that would be a bug.
8. At least three test cases in category 7 such that you have tried all three permutations where the length of one side is equal to the length of the sum of the other two sides	For example 1, 2, 3; 1, 3, 2; 3, 1, 2.
9. Three integers greater than zero such that the sum of two of the numbers is less than the third	For example 1, 2, 4 or 12, 15, 30.
10. At least three test cases in category 9 such that you have tried all three permutations	For example 1, 2, 4; 1, 4, 2; and 4, 1, 2.
11. All sides zero.	
12. Noninteger values.	
13. Wrong number of values	For example two more than three.
14. Did you specify expected output for each test case?	

REFERENCE

[1]   Myers, G. J., *The Art of Software Testing*, New York: Wiley, 1976

Appendix J

Software reliability models

This appendix lists the basic assumptions of the following models:

- Jelinski-Moranda model;
- Geometric model;
- Schick-Wolverton model;
- Goel-Okumoto nonhomogeneous Poisson process;
- Generalized Poisson model;
- Brooks-Motley model.

This information is derived from a lecture sponsored by the Boston section of the IEEE Reliability Group titled "Software Reliability Measurement, Assessment, and Modeling," presented by Dr. Michael Elbert and Dr. David Heimann, October-November 1991.

J.1 Jelinski-Moranda model

- There is a finite number of faults in the program.
- The failure rate $Z(t)$ is directly proportional to the number of remaining errors as follows:

$$Z(t) = K(\mathcal{N} - (i - 1))$$

where:

$\mathcal{N}$ = the number of initial errors.

i = the number of errors already detected and corrected.

K = a constant $Z(t)$ reduction coefficient.

K and $\mathcal{N}$ are unknown.

- The failure rate $Z(t)$ is constant until an error is corrected, at which time $Z(t)$ is again constant but at a reduced value.
- All errors are independent of each other and equally likely to occur.
- Each fault contributes equally to the unreliability of the program.
- Reliability growth occurs as a result of fixing faults.
- Faults are corrected instantaneously.
- Fixes are perfect and do not introduce new faults.
- All faults are of the same severity.

J.2 Geometric model

- There is an infinite number of total errors (i.e., the program will never be error free).
- All errors do not have the same chance of detection (i.e., all errors are not equally likely to occur).
- The error detection rate forms a geometric progression and is constant between error occurrences.
- Software is tested in a manner similar to the operational usage.
- The detection of errors is independent.

- The hazard rate function $Z(t)$ is computed as:

$$Z(t)=(d)(k)^{i-1}$$

where:

d = the initial hazard rate

k = a coefficient

The hazard rate function is initially a constant (d) that decreases in a geometric progression ($0 < k < 1$).

J.3   Schick-Wolverton model

- The hazard rate is proportional not only to the number of errors in the program but also to the amount of testing time. The chance of error detection increases with increasing testing time.
- All errors are equally likely to occur.
- The errors are corrected instantaneously without introduction of new errors.
- The software is tested in a manner similar to actual usage.
- Each error is of the same order of severity.
- The hazard rate function $Z(t)$ is calculated as:

$$Z(t_i) = k(n - (i-1))t$$

where:

ti = the amount of testing time between the $(i-1)$st error and the ith error.

k = the proportionality constant

n = the total number of errors in the program

J.4   Goel-Okumoto nonhomogeneous poisson process

- The cumulative number of faults detected at time t is Poisson-distributed with mean $m(t)$.
- The mean number of detected faults $m(t)$ is bounded and nondecreasing and approaches a limit a.
- The mean number of detected faults in a small time interval is proportional to the mean number of undetected faults, with constant of proportionality.
- There is a finite number of faults; therefore,

$$\Pr = \frac{m(t)e^{-m(t)}}{n!}$$

where Pr is the probability of n faults being detected in time t and

$$m(t) = a(1-e^{-bt})$$

J.5   Generalized poisson model

- A generalization of the Jelinski-Moranda or Schick-Wolverton models, taken in a framework of error count per interval.
- The expected number of errors is proportional to the fault content at time of testing and to some function of the amount of time spent in testing.
- Not all faults are necessarily corrected upon detection.
- Fault correction takes place at the end of intervals, without the introduction of new faults.
- Let $E(f_i)$ be the expected number of faults detected during the i-th time interval. Then:

$$E(f_i) = t \, [\mathcal{N} - M_{i-1}] \, g_i \, (x_1, x_{2,,,} \ldots, x_i)$$

where:

$\mathcal{N}$ = the initial number of faults.

M_{i-1} = the faults corrected after $i - 1$ time intervals.

t = proportionality constant.

$g_i(x_1, x_2,,, \ldots, x_i)$ is a function of the time spent testing.

J.6   Brooks-Motley model

- New faults can be introduced when existing faults are corrected.
- The number of new faults is proportional to the number of faults corrected.
- The number of faults detected is proportional to the number of faults at risk for detection, which in turn is proportional to the number of remaining faults.

$$n_i = (N - aN_{i-1})q$$

where:

n_i = the number of faults detected during the $(i-1)$th interval.

N = the number of faults in the program.

N_{i-1} = the number of faults detected through the $(i-1)$th interval.

a = the probability of correction without inserting new faults.

q = the error detection probability.

About the Author

S TEVEN R. RAKITIN received a B.S.E.E. from Northeastern University and an M.S.C.S. from Rennselaer Polytechnic Institute. He has 25 years of experience as a software engineer and a software quality professional in a broad range of industries, including nuclear power, defense, medical, and electronic design automation. He is a certified software quality engineer (CSQE) and a certified quality auditor (CQA) and is a member of the IEEE Computer Society and the American Society for Quality Control (ASQC).

Index

Recent Titles in the Artech House Computing Library

Internet and Intranet Security, Rolf Oppliger

Managing Computer Networks: A Case-Based Reasoning Approach, Lundy Lewis

Metadata Management for Information Control and Business Success, Guy Tozer

Multimedia Database Management Systems, Guojun Lu

Practical Guide to Software Quality Management, John W. Horch

Practical Process Simulation Using Object-Oriented Techniques and C++, José Garrido

Risk Management Processes for Software Engineering Models, Marian Myerson

Secure Electronic Transactions: Introduction and Technical Reference, Larry Loeb

Software Process Improvement With CMM, Joseph Raynus

Software Verification and Validation: A Practitioner's Guide, Steven R. Rakitin

Solving the Year 2000 Crisis, Patrick McDermott

User-Centered Information Design for Improved Software Usability, Pradeep Henry

For further information on these and other Artech House titles, including previously considered out-of-print books now available through our In-Print-Forever® (IPF®) program, contact:

Artech House
685 Canton Street
Norwood, MA 02062
Phone: 781-769-9750
Fax: 781-769-6334
e-mail: artech@artechhouse.com

Artech House
46 Gillingham Street
London SW1V 1AH UK
Phone: +44 (0)20 7596-8750
Fax: +44 (0)20 7630-0166
e-mail: artech-uk@artechhouse.com

Find us on the World Wide Web at:
www.artechhouse.com